D1539646

MAR 0 4 2013

HEROES OF
RACING

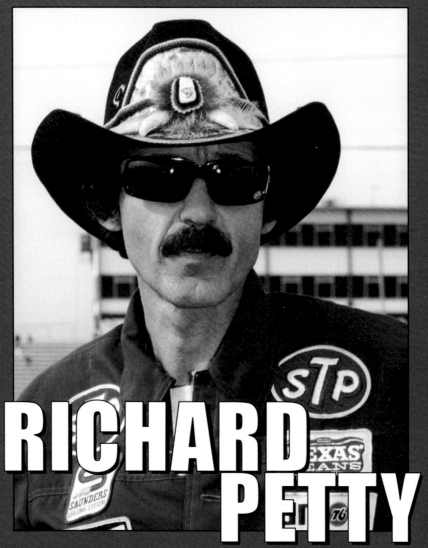

RICHARD
PETTY

The King of Racing

by J Chris Roselius

Enslow Publishers, Inc.
40 Industrial Road
Box 398
Berkeley Heights, NJ 07922
USA
http://www.enslow.com

Library of Congress Cataloging-in-Publication Data
Roselius, J Chris.
  Richard Petty : the king of racing / J Chris Roselius.
      p. cm. — (Heroes of racing)
  Summary: "A biography of American NASCAR driver Richard Petty"—Provided by publisher.
  Includes bibliographical references and index.
  ISBN-13: 978-0-7660-3298-9
  ISBN-10: 0-7660-3298-1
  1. Petty, Richard—Juvenile literature. 2. Automobile racing drivers—United States—Biography—Juvenile literature. I. Title.
  GV1032.P47R67 2009
  796.72092—dc22
  [B]
                                                           2008007693

Printed in the United States of America

10 9 8 7 6 5 4 3 2 1

To Our Readers: We have done our best to make sure all Internet addresses in this book were active and appropriate when we went to press. However, the author and the publisher have no control over and assume no liability for the material available on those Internet sites or on other Web sites they may link to. Any comments or suggestions can be sent by e-mail to comments@enslow.com or to the address on the back cover.

Disclaimer: This publication is not affiliated with, endorsed by, or sponsored by NASCAR. NASCAR®, WINSTON CUP®, NEXTEL CUP, BUSCH SERIES and CRAFTSMAN TRUCK SERIES are trademarks owned or controlled by the National Association for Stock Car Auto Racing, Inc., and are registered where indicated.

♻ Enslow Publishers, Inc. is committed to printing our books on recycled paper. The paper in every book contains 10% to 30% post-consumer waste (PCW). The cover board on the outside of each book contains 100% PCW. Our goal is to do our part to help young people and the environment too!

Photo credits: George Rose/Getty Images, 1; Eddie Malone/AP Images, 4; Jim Kerlin/AP Images, 8; AP Images, 15, 20, 22, 29, 31, 35, 55, 56, 61, 70, 80, 92; Whitehead/AP Images, 45; Foley/AP Images, 49; Cathie Rowand/Journal-Gazette/AP Images, 63; Chris O'Meara/AP Images, 76; Ira Schwarz/AP Images, 89; Phil Coale/AP Images, 90; Chuck Burton/AP Images, 97; Petty Enterprises/AP Images, 105; Erik Perel/AP Images, 106.

Cover Photo: George Rose/Getty Images

CONTENTS

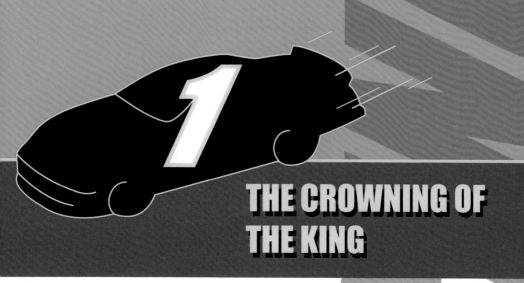

THE CROWNING OF THE KING

On a hot July afternoon in Nashville, Tennessee, Richard Petty was doing what he did best, racing his car around a track in an effort to prove he was the best driver. Petty was zooming around the track, holding off his nearest competitors, when his car suddenly started to shake. It appeared Petty's day had come to a premature end when he suffered a blown tire, a blowout that caused Petty to crash into the wall. Most people, including Petty's crew,

Former NASCAR driver Richard Petty at the 2008 Sprint Sound & Speed on January 12, 2008, in Nashville, Tennessee

assumed his chances of winning the race had disappeared.

The front end was knocked out of alignment and the car's rear spring was broken. That is not a good thing for any car, much less one traveling at speeds well over 150 miles per hour (241 kilometers per hour). Seeing the destruction, his crew was ready to tell Petty to park the car. But Petty wouldn't listen. He made a simple order—he told the crew to fix it. By the time the car was ready to take the track once again, Petty was ten laps behind the leader. Rocketing back onto the track, Petty chased down each car ahead of him one by one. By the end of the race, Petty not only had caught up to the rest of the field, he overtook everyone and claimed the victory. He won by a whopping five laps over the second-place finisher.

As amazing as the race was, it is just a sample of the complete dominance Richard Petty displayed over his competitors on the track in 1967.

DID YOU KNOW?

Petty married his wife, Lynda, in 1959 when he was twenty-two and she was only seventeen. They kept the marriage a secret for a while as she attended Randleman High School for her senior year and was named homecoming queen.

FROM ROCKET TO KING

Every sport has milestones athletes try to reach in a

season. For baseball, it is surpassing 100 runs batted in. In football, it is 1,000 yards rushing for a running back. These are numbers that are hard to reach but, at the same time, attainable. What Richard Petty did in 1967 during the NASCAR Grand National season, however, is incomprehensible. In fact, it will be nearly impossible for another NASCAR driver to ever match the season Petty had, much less come close to it.

RICHARD PETTY FILE

Birth date:
July 2, 1937

Years in NASCAR:
1958–1992

Career earnings:
$7,755,409

Nickname: The King

Personal: Married to Lynda; father to Kyle, Sharon, Lisa, and Rebecca.

Petty had turned in the most dominating performance the sport of NASCAR has ever seen. From the start of the season to the end, all Petty did was win—a lot. Of the forty-eight races that season, Petty won an astounding twenty-seven of them, or an unbelievable 56 percent of the races. Eight times in 1967 Petty was unable to finish a race. In the races he was able to finish, only once did Petty fail to finish in the top ten.

Richard Petty holds the trophy after winning the Daytona 500 on February 23, 1964.

Winning wasn't unusual for Petty. The native of Randleman, North Carolina, was an experienced and accomplished driver by the time the 1967 season rolled around. Petty claimed his first career NASCAR win on February 28, 1960, his third season as a NASCAR driver but first season racing the circuit full-time.

Petty took the track nine times in 1958, his rookie season. He then entered twenty-one of the forty-four races in 1959 before competing in forty of the forty-four races in 1960. Petty finished the 1960 season ranked second in the points standings.

He followed that with an overall finish of eighth in 1961 and then had back-to-back second-place finishes in 1962 and 1963. He finally broke through in 1964, claiming the points championship after a season in which he won nine races and finished in the top ten forty-three times. So NASCAR fans were used to seeing Petty in the winner's circle. But they were not used to seeing one driver there twenty-seven times! It is that amazing run through the 1967 campaign that led Petty to earn the nickname "The King." The nickname stuck.

"A bunch of reporters got together, sitting around . . . and got to talkin'," Petty said. "If my name had been Dale or Kyle or Darrell, it wouldn't have sounded like much. I mean, King Dale? But Richard was just a natural to go with King. They just [threw] it in there. They'd been trying to name me the Randle-man Rocket, all kinds of names. Never took hold. But first time anybody saw King Richard, it stuck."[1]

Benny Parsons, who won the points title in 1973 and raced for years against Petty, said Petty was more than just the King on the track. He was also one of the top drivers when it came to selling NASCAR to the fans.

DID YOU KNOW?

Petty set a NASCAR record by winning twenty-seven races in 1967. His ten straight wins that season is also a NASCAR record.

Knowing the sport needed all the media coverage it could get, Petty was available to the press.

"Petty was the man. He was the star," Parsons said. "He was the guy that every writer and every radio guy went up to talk to. The other drivers were capable, but everyone wanted Petty."[2]

SLOW START TO THE SEASON

Racing under a different schedule compared to NASCAR today, the 1967 season actually started in 1966. But that didn't matter to Petty. All he cared about was winning, and he started to rack up the victories from the very start of the season. On November 13, 1966, the Grand National season got underway with Petty starting in the third position at the Augusta 300. He didn't stay there long, however. In no time, Petty sped past the competition and into the lead, a lead he would basically hold the entire day. Petty held the lead for a total of 223 of the race's 300 laps. It was a great start to the season, but it would be one of only two wins Petty would earn in the first nine races of the season.

One of the reasons for the lack of wins was Petty's inability to finish a race. At the Motor Trend 500 in the second week of the season, Petty was forced to leave early when he experienced radiator problems. In February at the Daytona 500, the sport's biggest race, Petty completed only 193 of the 200 laps due to engine trouble. Petty's fortune changed during the following race in Weaverville, North Carolina. Not happy with the way his car was running after the Daytona 500, Petty changed from his 1967 Plymouth to the 1966 model, making minor adjustments to make it look like the 1967 model. The move worked. He easily won the Fireball 300, leading for 150 of the 300 laps on the half-mile track.

The thrill of victory, however, quickly disappeared as the following four races brought nothing but heartache to Petty and his crew. He crashed in two straight races, leaving him with finishes of thirty-fourth and nineteenth before placing second in Winston-Salem, North Carolina. Petty, however, was unable to finish the next race at Atlanta when engine problems forced him out. Through the first ten races of the 1967 season, Petty had only two wins. With the season moving into April, nobody expected to see what unfolded over the next seven months.

ONE WIN AFTER ANOTHER

During the first week of April, Petty and the rest of the NASCAR drivers gathered in Columbia, South Carolina, for the Columbia 200. Starting second after a great qualifying run, Petty and Jim Paschal traded the lead through the first seventy-nine laps of the race.

But after Petty zipped past Paschal on the eightieth lap, Petty's No. 43 car never looked back. He did not relinquish the lead over the final 120 laps. Paschal finished second, one full lap behind Petty, while Dick Hutcherson placed third, two laps behind Petty.

The win would be the start of one of the most amazing stretches of racing any NASCAR fan has ever witnessed. Petty started a run in which he won twenty-five of the next thirty-six races. He also had a string of seventeen straight top-ten finishes and fourteen straight top-four finishes. It didn't matter where Petty was racing, the length of the race, or if he was racing on dirt or a paved track. Petty simply dominated his opponents. After winning the Carolina 500 in Rockingham, North Carolina, on June 18, Petty passed James Hylton, who had yet to win a race, to claim the Grand National points lead. That lead increased with another win at Greenville, South Carolina, in addition to one third-place finish and one second-place finish.

What was it about Petty that made him so dominant on the track? What was the secret to his amazing success? According to fellow drivers, it was Petty's desire to always try to go faster that enabled him to beat the competition on such a consistent basis.

"Petty was the first guy on the track to hunt for that new groove," Parsons said. "He was the first guy to go up top—the first guy to go somewhere where the other cars weren't running—just to make his car faster."[3]

On July 4, 1967, after three months of finishing no worse than seventh in any race, Petty finally had a "bad" day at the track when he placed eleventh in the Firecracker 400. But the finish was only a small bump in the road for Petty and his team. He was back in Victory Lane at the next race in Trenton, New Jersey, and reeled off four wins and one second-place finish in the following five races. Engine problems forced Petty out of the race in Atlanta and left him in seventeenth place. It would be the last time Petty failed to win a race for nearly three months.

Starting on August 12, Petty went on a record ten-race winning streak. After winning the Myers Brothers 250 in Winston-Salem, in which he led the

INSIDE THE NUMBERS
In less than a decade on the NASCAR circuit, Petty broke his father's career record for victories when he claimed his fifty-fifth win in 1967.

race from start to finish, Petty didn't lose again until October 15. In six of those races, he started from the pole position and he held the lead for 1,781 of 2,931 laps during his winning streak. By the end of the season, Petty had 42,472 points to claim the overall title. Hylton finished in second place, 6,028 points behind the leader.

"Nobody has the patience to be Richard Petty," Buddy Baker, a former competitor against Petty, said about today's drivers compared to Petty. "He was in an era [when] he understood that public opinion meant whether you made the sport or not. And he had the ability to make it in the racetrack also. I don't think anybody that I see on the track right now resembles anything close."[4]

Petty's remarkable season brought unprecedented media coverage to the sport. Instead of being buried in the back of the sports section of newspapers, NASCAR races became front-page news as everyone was wondering if Petty won again. *Newsweek* devoted a story to Petty; it was the first time the weekly magazine ever had an article about a stock car driver. *Sports Illustrated* and *Life* magazines also had articles about Petty.

With a sincere attitude to go with his bright and easy-going smile, Petty gained a loyal following of fans, a loyalty he returned by allowing the media to do

Richard Petty clocked the fastest lap ever at the Daytona 500 during a practice run in 1968, reaching more than 186 m.p.h.

stories about him. While a few drivers and fans grumbled about all of the attention Petty was receiving, the driver born in a small town in North Carolina was now a fan favorite and a national sensation.

"I know of no other driver in NASCAR history who has brought more recognition to the sport," said NASCAR founder Bill France, Sr. "I can't agree with those who think Richard has gained more than his share. In bringing the spotlight into focus on the Petty team, he is also bringing added recognition to NASCAR. They have worked many years to achieve success. I'm proud he has set his records as a member of NASCAR."[5]

FOLLOWING HIS FATHER'S FOOTSTEPS

Richard Petty didn't grow up in the lap of luxury. Born on July 2, 1937 in Level Cross, North Carolina, Richard spent many of his childhood years in a house that didn't have electricity, running water, or a telephone. But Richard didn't think he was poor since most of his friends grew up in a similar fashion.

It wasn't an easy era. World War II made it tough on everyone in the early 1940s. But Richard had the love of his father, Lee, and mother, Elizabeth, and enjoyed playing with his brother, Maurice, as well as his friends. Many afternoons were spent riding his bike.

Lee Petty drove a delivery truck to support his family. But in the late 1930s, Lee Petty and his brother got involved in car racing on deserted roads late at night. The races weren't legal, but that didn't stop Lee Petty from becoming hooked. Any thoughts of racing, however, were pushed aside during World War II.

In 1947, a couple of years after the end of the war, racing was back on the mind of Lee Petty, and at the age of thirty-five, he began racing cars. In an effort to promote the sport and try to make racing safer for the drivers, a promoter named Bill France helped form NASCAR, and the first scheduled races started in 1949. Lee Petty decided to quit his job and became a professional race car driver. That decision changed Richard's future.

"My father was a jack-of-all-trades. Before he went into the racing business, he had a couple of trucks; he'd haul anything for anybody, anywhere, any-time—you know, one of those kinds of deals," Petty said. "And then, in 1949, he hung out in a service station in Greensboro, and he read in the paper where Bill France was having a strictly stock-car race in Charlotte. And he said, 'Hmmm. We're going to try that.' That's how it got started."[1]

LEARNING AT AN EARLY AGE

NASCAR looked completely different when it first started. Superspeedways were unheard of. Racing occurred on small tracks, usually on unpaved dirt tracks. The race in Daytona, which is home of the Daytona 500, was held on the beach.

The drivers, however, didn't care. For them, the ability to get out and race against fellow drivers was all that mattered. Competition is what Lee thrived on. Richard saw the joy racing brought to his father, and soon, both he and his brother were involved in their dad's profession. Lee had built a little machine shop, which was basically a fancy tool shed.

Before Richard was even in high school, he spent most of his weekends and hours after school working with his father in the machine shop. It wasn't long before Richard was a top-notch mechanic along with Maurice and their cousin, Dale Inman. The three boys traveled with Lee to the track on the weekends and served as the pit crew. They were in charge of filling the tank with gas, changing the tires, and making any adjustments the car needed during the race.

HE SAID IT

"If you're 100 percent confident, go, but if you're 95 percent confident, don't, because you'll get in trouble."

— Richard Petty

"I always compare my family to a farming family. My father was in the racing business instead of being a farmer," Petty said. "When I grew up, I started in the racing business instead of milking cows. We used to go to school and play football, baseball, and basketball, and all the boys, when they'd get through, they'd go home—most of them [were] country boys, and they'd plow fields and milk cows. I went home and worked on race cars."[2]

During his high school years at Randleman High, Richard was a good athlete. He played football, basketball, and baseball. But Richard was happy working with his dad on the weekends, and he believed he would become a mechanic when he grew older. When Richard graduated from high school, he went to work for Petty Enterprises and for his father full-time. With Lee's knowledge about building cars and Richard helping his father and learning all he could about cars, Lee became one of the top drivers on the Grand National circuit, the top level of NASCAR at the time.

HE SAID IT
"When I first started racing, my father, one of the first things he said, he said, 'Win the race as slow as you can.'"

— Richard Petty

Lee Petty (center) and his sons Maurice (left) and Richard look into the empty engine well of a new race car on July 15, 1964.

Richard Petty poses outside his race car in 1959.

For a while, Richard was content to help work on the cars. Richard, however, was an athlete, and he missed the thrill and excitement of competing against other people like he did in high school. One day, Richard was driving a car on the test track. Being behind the wheel and experiencing the excitement of handling a fast car, Richard realized what he wanted to be. He wanted to be like his dad and race cars.

DID YOU KNOW?

Petty's NASCAR career was delayed for several years due to his father insisting that Petty wait until he was twenty-one before he competed in a NASCAR race.

Lee was not thrilled with Richard's sudden realization, so he made a deal with his son. Lee said Richard could become a race car driver, but he would have to wait until his twenty-first birthday. Lee felt the wait would end Richard's quest to become a driver. But after waiting for three years, Richard turned twenty-one. Soon after his birthday, the younger Petty approached his father and asked if he could race.

BIRTH OF A RACER

On July 12, 1958, Richard was given his shot at proving himself on the track. Given a used 1957 convertible by Lee, Richard and his brother headed to Columbia and its dirt track. Competing against older and more experienced drivers, Richard not only survived his first race, but he finished sixth, earning $200.

"I was not trying to win that first race," Richard said. "I just wanted to finish and I was looking for a driving style that would be comfortable for me.

That was the first time I ever got in a race car and went tearing down into the corner to see how hard I could go. I felt comfortable with it."[3]

With his sixth-place finish, Richard was more certain than ever that racing cars was what he was supposed to do in his life. The $200 payday was nice, but the competition is what fueled Richard's desire to race. With his father providing the car, Richard entered his first Grand National race only six days after his success in Columbia.

DID YOU KNOW?

Petty's father, Lee, was one of the top drivers in NASCAR during his career, winning three Grand National titles and holding the career record for victories before Richard surpassed his total in 1967.

Driving an Oldsmobile with the number 142 on the side, Richard competed in Toronto at the Canadian National Exposition track. He lasted fifty-five laps before crashing into the fence, knocking him out of the race.

The crash, however, wasn't entirely Richard's fault. His father played a part in the accident.

"It wasn't much of a race," Richard recalled. "I got in Daddy's way when he was lapping me, so he punted me into the fence. He went on to win, so I reckon it was a good day for the Pettys."[4]

Richard entered eight more races that season and proved he was more than capable of racing against the other drivers. He finished eleventh in his second race and then came in ninth in his third race. He was able to finish two more races he entered, but also suffered one crash and didn't finish three other races due to problems with the car.

"I was so cocky from that first race that I think I wrecked in my next three races," Richard said, slightly exaggerating his early problems on the track. "I learned to drive by driving. There is no school where someone can teach you on the blackboard. You have to get in that car and hit the walls and find out all about it for yourself."[5]

Richard's early enrollment into the school of driving paid off. During the 1959 season, the rookie would leave no doubt that he would be a driver to keep an eye on.

"**R**ichard, if you expect to make it in anything, you gotta put all you've got into it. . . . You have to work harder than the next guy if you expect to be a success."[1] That advice, uttered to Petty by his father, was on full display in 1959.

The brief exposure Petty got on the racetrack in 1958 helped pave the way for a successful rookie season in 1959. He was able to take everything he learned by watching his dad, combine it with his own experience behind the wheel, and find a winning formula. At the tender age of twenty-two, Petty entered twenty-one of the forty-four races, and in nearly each race, he drove like a veteran. He wasn't experienced enough to take the checkered flag in any of his races, but his confidence and ability allowed him to finish in the top five six times and rack up nine top-ten finishes.

Petty came close to his first Grand National victory in Atlanta when he placed second out of a forty-car field. He also had three third-places finishes. Those results gave Petty a fifteenth-place finish in the overall standings. He was also named the Rookie of the Year. Petty actually thought he had earned the win at the Lakewood Speedway in Atlanta until another driver protested, saying the laps were miscounted. It turns out that driver, Lee Petty, was correct, allowing him to earn the victory and forcing young Richard to settle for second place.

The 1959 season also was the first running of the Daytona 500 on the brand new, two-and-a-half-mile superspeedway that was built with the intention of giving NASCAR a signature race. The Daytona International Speedway was constructed six miles from the beach, where

DID YOU KNOW?

Petty, his brother Maurice, and cousin Dale Inman served as Lee Petty's pit crew before Richard became a driver himself.

races used to be run on the sand and nearby road. The track was huge, with high-banked turns and a giant grandstand. Petty remembers the first time he saw the massive track.

"We came through the tunnel and I think there was one building in the infield, they had enough grandstand up there for maybe 20–25,000 people, and it looked like it was forever down to the first corner because there was nothing there," Petty said. "Johnny Bruner was the NASCAR flagman at the time and nobody had ever been on the track with any stock cars. He said, 'OK, I want everybody to go out and run around on the flat for four or five laps before you ever even get up on the bank. We just want you to get used to the surroundings,' because it was so big.

"So I go out in my little convertible, run through the first and second corner, then the third and fourth corner. I think, 'Hmmm. OK.' I got up on the bank, come back around again and he's got the black flag out for me—so I'm officially the first black-flag guy here."[2]

After waiting out some rain in the days prior to the race, the Daytona 500 got underway with Petty starting in the sixth position. But that would be the best thing he would experience in the race. Driving an old 1957 Oldsmobile convertible, Petty lasted eight

Richard Petty recorded his third victory in the thirteen-year history of the Daytona 500 in 1971.

laps before his engine had trouble and led to an early exit. But the time Petty spent at Daytona proved to be a valuable learning experience. For one thing, he learned how to set up a car for the faster tracks.

"As a 21-year-old kid, the whole [racing] world was new to me," Petty said. "I'd only run 10–12 races before I went to Daytona. The fastest we'd been was to Darlington [S.C.] at around 100 mph [160 kph]. We could run about 130 mph [209 kph], like we did in the 100-mile [160-km] [qualifying race] that first year. I was OK running 130, but when they started the main race, all of a sudden the front cars were running 145. I jumped in with them at 145 till it sucked the motor out of it. We came to find we needed to change gears in the car to make it work."[3]

Petty and the rest of the drivers also got an early lesson in how to draft and how a car reacts to drafting. When a lead car breaks through the wind, a trailing car has less resistance and then has the ability to gain speed easier to make a pass.

"It kind of started dawning on people that something was happening, though they didn't know why or how," Petty said.[4]

DID YOU KNOW?

Petty earned only $760 dollars in his first year of racing in 1958, an average of just more than $84 per race.

BREAKOUT SEASON

In 1960, Petty firmly established himself as one of the top drivers in NASCAR. The young driver was now racing full-time as he competed in forty of the forty-four races. After starting the season with a twelfth-place finish at Charlotte and then a sixth-place showing at Columbia, Petty and his crew headed to Daytona for the big 500-mile (804-km) race. Petty entered the race feeling good about his car, but after what happened in 1959, he was hoping engine trouble wouldn't sideline him once again.

Richard Petty crawls out of his race car at Daytona International Speedway in 1975.

It never did. Starting nineteenth in the field, Petty handled his car beautifully and soared past the cars in front of him. In fact, Petty battled for the lead throughout the race, holding the lead for a total of twenty-nine laps. Petty wasn't able to hold on and win the race, but he showed his skill by finishing third, one spot ahead of his father. Petty wasn't able to break through at Daytona, but he wasted no time to finally notch his first career victory. Competing against twenty other drivers at Charlotte on February 28, Petty started the race in seventh place and methodically moved ahead of the cars in front of him.

The race eventually became a battle between Rex White and Petty. Trying to fight each other off, Petty was able to overtake White and then held on for the win, the first of his 200 career victories. The race would be symbolic of the season to come, as White and Petty ended up competing for the overall title. Petty went on to win two more races in 1960 and recorded sixteen top-five finishes and thirty top-ten showings. White, however, was a little better, claiming six wins, twenty-five top-five showings and thirty-five top-ten finishes. In the end, White won the overall title with 21,164

HITTING THE TRACK
One day after his twenty-first birthday, Petty competed in a race near Columbia, North Carolina, and finished sixth.

points, while Petty came in second with 17,228. Considering the 1960 season was Petty's first as a full-time driver, his second-place finish was astonishing.

TRAGEDY AND MISFORTUNE

Petty entered the 1961 season full of confidence coming off his second-place overall finish the previous year. But in 1961,

DID YOU KNOW?

Petty was named the Rookie of the Year in 1959 after finishing in the top ten nine times and the top five six times in twenty-one starts.

nothing seemed to go right for Petty, starting with the first race of the season in Charlotte and ending with the final race in Hillsboro. The season-opening race resulted in an eleventh-place finish, as Petty completed only 142 of the 200 laps due to a problem with the car's frame. Petty's luck appeared to change the following race in Jacksonville when he finished in fourth place, but his luck ran out once he got to Daytona.

As part of earning a spot in the Daytona 500 field, the drivers had to compete in one of two forty-lap qualifying races. On February 24, two days before the big race, Petty was competing in the first qualifying race. Everything was going smoothly until the fortieth and final lap. As Petty entered Turn 1, he bumped into Junior Johnson. When Johnson's car blew a tire, he started to spin out of control. Petty was caught up in the hectic moment as Johnson's car smashed into the right rear corner of Petty's car.

Unable to control his own car, Petty slammed into the reinforced guard rail at the top of the track. The force of the collision lifted the front of the car onto the rail, where it rode along the top of it for several hundred yards. Suddenly, the car was lifted into the air and catapulted into the parking lot before landing on the ground with a thud.

Amazingly, Petty crawled out of the badly damaged car with only a small cut and a sprained ankle, which he suffered while trying to get away from the wreckage. However, after experiencing pain in his eyes after the incident, medical personnel found tiny bits of glass particles in Petty's eyes. Petty's crash, however, wouldn't compare to what happened in the second qualifying race.

In a stunning turn of events, Lee Petty was involved in a horrific crash with John Beauchamp in nearly the same place Richard Petty had crashed earlier in the day. Lee Petty and Beauchamp both hit the outside guard rail and flew into the air. Lee Petty's car finally came back down with a thud, just feet from where Richard Petty had landed. At first glance, the younger Petty thought his father was dead. Somehow, Lee was still alive, and after being cut out of the car, he was rushed to Halifax Hospital, where he slipped in and out of consciousness for the next few days. Both Lee and Richard missed the running of the Daytona 500 as the entire family stayed with Lee in the hospital.

Lee would eventually get better and compete on the track, but the crash effectively ended his career. During his stay in the hospital, Lee told his sons, Richard and Maurice, and their cousin, Dale Inman, to head back to the shop in Level Cross and rebuild the cars. During their time in Level Cross, the cars were rebuilt, but with a twist. One car was built to

Junior Johnson peers from his car after winning the pole position for the Dixie 400 stock car race in 1964.

THE BIRTH OF "PETTY BLUE"

Late in the 1959 season, Petty and his brother Maurice were rebuilding their car when Maurice said they didn't have enough white paint to cover the entire car.

Petty found some dark blue paint and they mixed the two paints together. The result was a striking blue.

They liked what they created, so they made sure to remember the right mix of paint. The "Petty Blue" color was born. It became a trademark of Petty's cars.

perform on short tracks, while the second car was designed to perform on high-speed tracks. Lee didn't race the rest of the season and climbed into his race car once in 1962, three times in 1963 and twice in 1964 before retiring from the sport he helped build. In a testament to his determination, Lee Petty finished fifth in his lone race in 1962.

Richard was able to return to the track in Spartanburg on March 4, 1961. Somehow, he was able to tune out the distraction that came with his first race since the awful events in Daytona to place second. By the end of the season, Petty notched two wins and had eighteen top-five finishes to finish eighth in the overall standings. It was an amazing showing considering the wreck he suffered and the fact that he was trying to help his father recover back home.

AT THE TOP OF HIS GAME

With Lee concentrating on rehabilitating himself, Richard assumed the lead role at Petty Enterprises. Under his leadership, the team became one of the best over the next three seasons. Competing in fifty-two races in 1962, Petty claimed eight victories and thirty-two top-five finishes. The results were good enough for a second-place finish in the standings, less than 2,000 points behind champion Joe Weatherly. Petty was even better in 1963, winning a career-high fourteen of the fifty-four races he entered. But once again, he fell just short of the overall title, and Weatherly won the championship. Petty, however, would finally break through in 1964.

The 1964 season opened with three top-five finishes in the first four races, including a win at Savannah. As February rolled around, it meant another trip to Daytona. Petty was tired of not winning what was quickly becoming the biggest race of the season. With his crew setting up his car just as he wanted it, Petty dominated the Daytona field during the race, leading for 184 of the 200 laps to win easily. He was the only driver to finish on the lead

DID YOU KNOW?

Petty competed in the very first Daytona 500 in 1959. He had to watch most of the race from pit row, however, after suffering a blown engine after only eight laps.

lap. Jimmy Pardue was second, one lap behind, while Paul Goldsmith and Marvin Panch finished third and fourth, two laps behind Petty.

Petty's talent was the main reason for him becoming one of the top drivers on the NASCAR circuit. But his equipment also helped. For the 1964 season, Petty drove a car with a massive 426-cubic-inch, Hemi-head Chrysler engine. The power it created was outstanding.

"The first time I cranked it," Petty said. "I thought it was gonna suck the hood into the engine."[5]

Petty said the Hemi engine played a large role in him claiming the Daytona 500.

"Chrysler brought out the Hemi engine, and I guess I just had more under the hood than anybody else," Petty said. "It was the first time that I could pull out and pass people and them not pass me right back. But it was not a deal where you just Cadillaced around and drove it easy. You drove the full 500 miles. It was probably ten or fifteen miles per hour faster than I had ever run, and I ran every lap just as hard as I could, and the deal of just being that fast with those little tires we had on them. They didn't have spoilers on the car, and we didn't have all the ground effects and stuff that they have now. So it was an armful all the time."[6]

Ironically, Petty's family wasn't on hand to witness his first Daytona 500 victory.

"When we won the race in '64, the kids all had the mumps or measles or something. There were three of them then—Kyle, Sharon, and Lisa. They didn't get to go to the race. The kids didn't even see me till I came back from the racetrack with a trophy. We've got a picture at home where we're sitting there on the bed with the kids all around the trophy in the motel room."[7]

Petty carried the success he had at Daytona into the rest of the season, claiming nine victories, thirty-seven top-five finishes, and forty-three top-ten finishes. Ned Jarrett also had an outstanding season, winning fifteen times and finishing forty races in the top five. But in the end, Petty held off Jarrett to claim his first Grand National points championship.

Petty's rivals, however, didn't like the advantage he got from his engine. Responding to the criticism, NASCAR banned the use of the engine for the 1965 season, leading to a standoff between Petty and NASCAR.

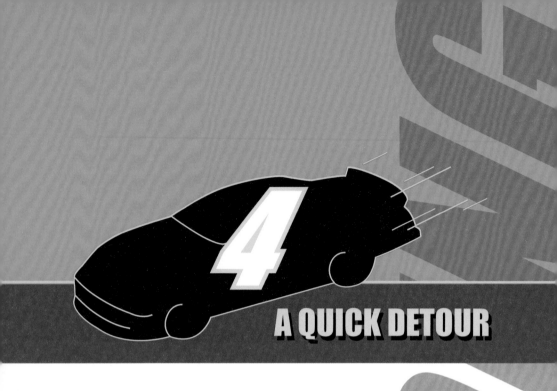

As the 1964 season unfolded, it was becoming clear that the Hemi engine in Petty's car was cranking out the power. However, since Petty and other Chrysler drivers were not used to that power, there was learning involved in just how to harness it. Several Chrysler drivers throughout the season were unable to finish races due to engine problems.

Petty, for the most part, was able to figure out how to harness the Hemi and race with it. As the season progressed, others started to believe Petty had an advantage, a belief that wasn't really true. While Petty did win the Grand National title, he was in a battle with two other drivers that season—Ned Jarrett, who drove a Ford, and David Pearson, who raced in a Dodge.

What really clinched the title for Petty was the fact that he entered all sixty-one races scheduled while Jarrett competed in fifty-nine. The extra points Petty gained in the two races Jarrett failed to enter helped push him toward the title.

Despite the thrilling competition between the drivers, Bill France, the NASCAR chief, changed the rules for the 1965 season. What he did had a big impact.

He outlawed the Hemi engine and the Ford "hi-riser" engine from NASCAR competitions in an effort to restrict the size and power of racing engines. France defended his decision by explaining that the change would also help the smaller teams who couldn't afford more expensive engines such as the Hemi.

"Stock car racing," France said, "has in recent years been in danger of being taken over completely by the big, wealthy companies. Cost of engines crept up from $1,000 to beyond $2,200. Manufacturers were constantly changing them—and on short notice—and turning out special engines to dominate racing. . . . The little independent stock car racers were being forced out of the picture."[1]

Ford didn't mind the rule change. It had threatened to not race in 1965 if the Hemi wasn't outlawed. Not surprisingly, Chrysler, which had cars place one-two-three in the 1964 Daytona 500, was upset.

"France made stock-car racing," groused a Chrysler mechanic. "Now he'll kill it."[2]

"Ridiculous. This is ridiculous," Ronnie Householder, who headed up racing activities for Chrysler, complained. "I don't think we are ever going to get together again. Now, look here. The idea of racing is to go fast. Right? It is elementary. Engine restrictions, my foot. I can't see where people will come out to watch cars run 150 miles an hour [241 kph] when they know there are cars that can go 175. Go fast. That's the idea. Another thing. France's rule about engines in volume production. I would like to point out that the Chrysler Corporation would like to decide for itself how many engines it is going to build and does not need any instructions from NASCAR."[3]

UNPLANNED SIDE TRIP

Ten days after the announcement from France, Chrysler issued a statement that Chrysler teams would not compete in any NASCAR event unless the rules were changed. France and NASCAR stuck to the new rules, leading Petty and other Chrysler-supported teams to other racing events.

"My espionage tells me that these rules are popular within the industry," France said. "And I think that in 1966 you will see more makes of cars back on the track."[4]

With Petty receiving money from Chrysler, he supported the decision to boycott NASCAR. So when the 1965 season started, Petty wasn't getting ready to defend his title. Instead, as NASCAR geared up for the Daytona 500, Petty was getting prepared for the start of the drag racing season, despite requests from other sponsors to drive for them on the NASCAR circuit.

"Oh, I've had offers from practically everybody to drive for them, to change sponsors," said Petty.

A REAL DRAG
After the Hemi engine was banned for the 1965 season, Petty honored the decision by Chrysler to boycott NASCAR races and instead tried his hand at drag racing.

"But I've been with Chrysler a long time, and I intend to stay with them. I'm just drag racing now because a guy has got to do something to stay in business.

"When we were stock car racing only, we sat around and put all our eggs in one basket. Then we got the basket pulled out from under us. Drag racing is all right. The money I make here is mostly profit, all right. But there isn't that excitement."[5]

While Petty stood by Chrysler's decision to boycott the NASCAR circuit, it was plain to see that he wanted to be back driving on the oval tracks he had come to dominate. He knew, however, that something would have to be worked out between NASCAR and Chrysler before he could return to the track. In the meantime, Ford was clearly the new king on the track.

"I don't know how much longer this ban will go on, but we're trying to get Chrysler and NASCAR back together before the year is over," Petty said.[6]

SUCCESS MIXED WITH SORROW

Driving a highly modified Plymouth Barracuda that featured the Hemi engine, Petty was a star on the drag racing circuit, bringing in fans all around the southern United States. The Barracuda was given the name "43 Junior," while a second Barracuda used by Petty was named "Outlawed," a joke toward NASCAR's ban against the Hemi. The first time Petty took the

Richard Petty wipes his face after wrapping up a victory.

"Outlawed" car out, he hit 140 miles per hour (225 kph) on the one-quarter mile (0.4 km) track. Just as he had done on the NASCAR tracks, Petty racked up the wins during the spring and summer.

Earlier in the season, however, Petty was involved in a horrible accident. During a race in Dallas, Georgia, at Southeastern Dragway, Petty had some

WELCOME BACK

After NASCAR relented on its ban of the Hemi engine midway through the 1965 season, Petty returned to compete in fourteen races and won four of them while finishing in the top five ten times overall.

DID YOU KNOW?

When Petty won the 1964 Grand National title, the Pettys became the first father-son champions in NASCAR history.

transmission problems coming off the starting line during a race against Arnie Beswick. Petty got the car into the gear he wanted, but the car got loose. Unable to get the car under control, Petty and the "Outlawed" headed right toward the grandstands.

The car hit the embankment and shot into the air, hurdling the protective fence and into the crowd. The car slammed into the spectators, injuring seven of them and killing an eighth person, an eight-year-old boy. While the wins were nice, they didn't help Petty overcome the tragedy, which haunted him for years.

NASCAR CHANGES ITS MIND

As the NASCAR season progressed, more and more fans stayed away from the track. Without Petty and a number of other popular drivers racing, the spectators decided it wasn't worth their time to watch only Ford and Mercury cars race. The lack of fans was only one of the problems France and NASCAR faced.

Track owners were upset, as were promoters and race car companies. All of them wanted the Chrysler drivers back. All of them wanted Petty back. With the future of NASCAR in doubt, France finally changed his mind and allowed the Hemi engine to be used during a NASCAR race. Hearing the good news, Petty quickly ended his career as a drag racer and returned to the NASCAR circuit. It wasn't long before he was back in the winner's circle.

In his first seven races back on the NASCAR circuit, Petty won twice, finished second twice and third twice. In fact, the only time Petty didn't finish a race in the top three was when he did not finish the event, which happened five times due to engine problems or a crash. In the other nine races, he finished no worse than third. Unfortunately for Petty, since he missed the first forty-one races of the season, it was impossible to catch the leaders in the points standings. He finished thirty-eighth overall, the worst finish in his career.

HE SAID IT

"You still remember it and still worry about it, but life goes on."
— Richard Petty

BACK WHERE
HE BELONGS

With the NASCAR-Chrysler feud over, Petty was allowed to focus all of his attention to upcoming 1966 season, and it showed in the first race of the year at Augusta. Starting from the pole position, Petty led for 132 laps en route to the victory. The following race wasn't as kind to Petty as he was forced to leave early due to engine problems in a race in Riverside, California.

The upcoming race, however, was what Petty really cared about. Sidelined from the Daytona 500 in

1965, Petty wanted to make sure everyone knew he was the one to beat in the 1966 race. To prove his point, Petty was at the track early, running one fast lap after another during practice in his No. 43 Plymouth.

"You're early, aren't you?" asked a reporter. "I'm a year late," Petty replied.[1]

His tone let everyone know he was in Daytona to do one thing and one thing only—go fast and win. He proved he could go fast, setting a new qualifying speed record of 175 miles per hour (281 kph). Now, he had to prove he could win.

Richard Petty waves from his car as he makes his way into Victory Lane following another Daytona 500 title.

As the big race approached, the drama and anticipation became more and more intense. The fans were ecstatic to see Petty back behind the wheel and looked forward to seeing the Chryslers and Fords once again battling on the track. The battle, however, never really materialized.

As is the tradition before the Daytona 500, twin qualifying races were held on Friday as a way to set up the racing order for the big event on Sunday. In the first race, Paul Goldsmith battled Petty to the wire, just edging the 1964 Daytona 500 champion to claim the win. Both drivers were in Chrysler Plymouth cars. Plymouth cars took first and second once again.

"We knew they were fast," said Leo Beebe, head of Ford's racing program, "but, wow! No matter how you try to steel yourself for these things they still come at you like—well, like death. Sudden and unexpected."[2]

On race day, the weather was gloomy, with the threat of rain poised to either postpone the race or possibly end it early. The weather cooperated and the race started on schedule. As was the case all week, Petty and Goldsmith looked to have the fastest cars as they bolted ahead of the rest of the field. Only twenty laps into the race, however, Petty's front left tire started to smoke.

The King was able to pit his car, and with amazing quickness, the crew quickly changed tires and had

POPULAR WITH THE DRIVERS

During his long career, Petty has always been popular with the fans. But he has also been popular with fellow drivers, earning the Most Popular Winston Cup Series Driver honor nine times, including a stretch of five straight years from 1974–1978.

Petty back on the track. The pit stop, however, cost him, because he was now racing with the rest of the field. It wouldn't be long before he put them in his rearview mirror.

"I guess we sat on the pole, and we were the quickest car all week long," Petty said after the race. "That car, again, like the '64 car, was just a real fast car, and we just outran everybody."[3]

As Petty soared past the rest of the drivers, he had a stranglehold on the race at its midway point. Unless he got involved in an accident or experienced engine problems, there was no doubt about who was going to win. By the time Petty crossed the finish line three laps early due to rain for the victory, he had held the lead for 108 laps.

"The only way you can win the race is to go wide open, so that's what we did," Petty said. "They called the race with three laps to go, so the only problem I had then was to make sure I didn't spin out from all the rain, because they went ahead and continued to run it [under yellow] even under a downpour."[4]

The rest of the season didn't go as smoothly for Petty. He was still one of the fastest drivers on the track every week, starting another thirteen races from the pole position. He won seven of those races. Five other times he didn't finish the race due to either a crash, engine problems, or car problems. Overall, Petty failed to finish sixteen of the thirty-nine races he entered, leading to a third place in the overall standings.

During the offseason, Petty and his crew worked on how to make sure his car finished more races. Crashes were going happen, but having to leave a race due to engine problems was never accepted. The goal for the 1967 season was to reduce the number of races not finished. That goal was accomplished.

One of the keys for Petty's once-in-a-lifetime 1967 season was the fact that he cut the number of "Did Not Finishes" in half, from sixteen to eight. Petty won only three more poles in 1967 than he did in 1966, but he won nineteen more races.

TRYING TO LIVE UP TO '67

It would have been silly to think Petty could duplicate his twenty-seven victories and ten-race winning streak in 1968. Petty, however, did his best to repeat that amazing performance. He started the season with a second-place showing in Macon and a victory in Montgomery. But he finished tenth at Riverside and then eighth at the Daytona 500, a disappointing finish for Petty.

Three more races produced finishes of second, seventeenth, and sixth before he finally got back to the winner's circle by claiming the win at Hickory. He followed that victory with another the next race, but Petty then went through a nine-race drought in which his best performance was a third-place finish at Weaverville and then Darlington. During that span, Petty did not finish six races. He had engine problems three times and issues with the rear end, axle, and ignition the other three races.

Over the final thirty-one races of the season, Petty looked more like his dominant self on the track. He won thirteen of those thirty-one races and finished in the top five another ten times. However, the No. 43 car still suffered its share of bad luck as Petty was forced to pit early in eight other races due to one problem or another. In those eight races, Petty finished no better than twenty-first. In the end, that helped keep

IF IT WASN'T PETTY, IT WAS PEARSON

From 1963–1977, Petty and rival David Pearson finished one-two in sixty-three races. Pearson won thirty-three of those races. Petty had the advantage on superspeedways during their career, earning fifty-five wins compared to fifty-one for Pearson.

Petty from defending his Grand National points title. He finished third overall.

The 1969 season was very similar to the '68 campaign. When Petty was able to finish a race, he usually did so in the lead or near the lead. He won ten races that season and had thirty-one top-five finishes. But Petty was unable to finish fifteen races. The loss of points in the races he was unable to finish cost Petty the points title. He finished second overall.

As the decade of the 1960s came to an end, Petty was clearly among NASCAR's best drivers and certainly was its most popular. Only thirty-two years old at the end of the 1969 season, Petty was already the all-time leader in career wins, had won two Daytona 500s, and claimed two Grand National titles. But Petty was only getting warmed up.

Richard Petty takes a break while preparing for the Purolator 500 in 1974.

Throughout the 1960s, Petty had proven himself to be one of the top drivers in NASCAR. He had two Grand National titles under his belt in addition to four second-place finishes and two third-place finishes. Petty also had two Daytona 500 titles. But "The King" raised his performance to another level during the first half of the 1970s. From 1970–1975, Petty won four of his record seven points titles and three of his record seven Daytona 500 races.

Richard Petty cools down after a day of practice for the Firecracker 400 in 1970.

After falling short of the overall title in 1969, Petty entered the 1970 season confident he could reclaim the points title he last won in 1967. The way the season started, it appeared Petty was poised to win his third title. He claimed four first-place finishes in the first eleven races, taking the checkered flag at Rockingham, Savannah, North Wilkesboro, and Columbia.

The victory at North Wilkesboro was an amazing performance. Petty struggled during qualifying and started the race sixteenth. But the No. 43 car was running as well as it had all season, and with Petty pushing the vehicle to go as fast as possible, he weaved his way through traffic so easily it appeared all of the other cars were just parked on the track. In seemingly the blink of an eye, Petty was in the lead. He wound up leading the race for 349 laps. He was nearly as dominant the next week in Columbia, when he led for 104 laps on his way to earning the victory.

Any hopes of challenging for the title, however, were put to an end when the circuit went to Darlington for the

DID YOU KNOW?

NASCAR had been making some big waves in high places. The President of the United States, Richard Nixon, invited many members of NASCAR to the White House in 1971. Richard Petty got to show his Plymouth to the president.

Rebel 400. In that race, Petty suffered a crash that nearly claimed his life. Coming out of Turn 4, Petty lost control of his car and, at nearly full speed, smashed head on into the inside concrete wall, actually breaking the wall where the car collided. The force of the impact spun the car sideways before it was tossed into the air and barrel-rolled down the racetrack.

Inside, Petty was tossed around. When the car finally came to a stop, Petty was hanging three-quarters of the way out of the driver's window. Somehow, amazingly, Petty avoided any life-threatening injuries. But he was banged up enough that he was forced to miss the next six races, effectively ending any hopes of winning the points championship.

When Petty returned to the track, he didn't need much time to get back into Victory Lane. Over the final twenty-eight races, Petty won 50 percent of them and had six other top-five finishes. For the season, he finished with 18 victories and 3,447 points. But those six missed races left too big of a deficit to overcome, and Bobby Isaac won the championship.

The 1971 season didn't start the way Petty would have liked. Engine troubles forced him out of the season-opening race at Riverside and led to a twentieth-place finish. That would be one of the few things that didn't go right for Petty that season, however.

From start to finish, he was clearly the best driver on the track. In only five of the season's forty-eight races did Petty fail to lead for at least one lap. The winning started at the Daytona 500. Battling teammate Buddy Baker and A. J. Foyt for much of the race, Petty pulled away to win the event by ten seconds and become the first driver to win the Daytona 500 three times.

"Buddy Baker was driving for us, and me, Buddy and A. J. Foyt had the three fastest cars," Petty said. "The deal was, Foyt was probably as quick or quicker than we were, but they made a pit stop and didn't get the car full of gas. Somehow, the gas tank didn't take the gas right and we got away from him. Anyhow, that was the time Petty Enterprises ran first and second."[1]

The victory was the first of twenty-one races Petty would win in 1971. It was a rare occurrence when Petty did not compete for the checkered flag. He notched thirty-eight top-five showings and forty-one top-ten finishes. Thanks to the sponsorship of Winston, which sponsored tracks in which races

THE MILLION DOLLAR MAN

In 1971, Petty became the first NASCAR driver to pass $1 million in career earnings. He won his third Daytona 500 that year, and added numbers four and five in 1973 and 1974.

were more than 250 miles that season, Petty also took home a lot more prize money than at any time in his career. During 1967, when he won his second Grand National title, Petty earned $130,000. In 1971, Petty earned $309,000 and in the process became the first NASCAR driver to reach more than $1 million in career earnings.

Of course, since the 1971 season seemed to go so smoothly, there had to be a bump in the road at some point. That bump came when Chrysler

Petty pulls into Victory Lane after the 1971 Daytona 500 at the Daytona International Speedway.

announced it would no longer be sponsoring any factory race teams. Petty Enterprises was left knowing they would have to find some new sponsorship for the 1972 season. Petty, however, always appeared to be thinking ahead. In 1970, he was able to get 7-Up, the soft drink maker, to be a sponsor for a few races. He was also able to get Pepsi Cola to sign up for sponsorship of a few races in 1971. With a history of being able to find sponsors, Petty was certain he could find a major sponsor for 1972.

BIG CHANGES IN THE OFFSEASON

During the offseason, Andy Granatelli contacted Petty at his home in Level Cross. Granatelli was president of Studebaker Technical Products, more famously known as STP. Granatelli had a lot of money and was looking for a racing team to sponsor. Petty, of course, wanted a sponsor who could provide him with a lot of money.

During a meeting in Chicago before the start of the season, Petty, along with his brother Maurice and cousin Dale Inman, negotiated a sponsorship deal with Granatelli. The discussions went smoothly, except in one area—the paint job for the car. Petty wanted to stick with his trademark Petty Blue. Granatelli wanted the cars to be his trademark Fluorescent Red. Petty came close to walking away from the deal until

Petty (left) and Andy Granatelli formed a business partnership in the 1970s that would last for years.

Granatelli offered a compromise. The cars would be painted with both colors. Thus was the birth of one of the most famous paint schemes in NASCAR history.

With financial backing taken care of, Petty was able to concentrate solely on winning in 1972, though how he won was a little different than past seasons. Winston and Bill France changed the look of how the 1972 campaign would unfold. The Grand National points system was thrown out and replaced with the Winston Cup series, in which all races were scored in six different categories. Dirt tracks were also eliminated as well as races that were less than 100 miles (161 km) long on paved tracks. The schedule was also reduced to only thirty-one races, ushering in the "modern era" of NASCAR racing.

The changes didn't affect Petty. He won the first race of the season at Riverside but then had a disastrous Daytona 500, as he finished twenty-sixth due to valve problems with the car. Petty was back in the winner's circle the next week and started a streak in which he placed no worse than sixth in the next nine races. The streak included two wins and the unveiling of a new look for Petty.

On May 7, 1972, Petty competed in the new STP Dodge Charger, which featured the STP logo. Petty finished fifth in the race, and for the rest of the season, he alternated between driving the Charger and the Plymouth Road Runner. In the final twenty-one races of the season, Petty drove the Dodge eleven times and the Plymouth ten times, experiencing more

THE ORIGINAL IRON MAN

Petty started a streak of competing in 513 straight Winston Cup races on November 14, 1971. The streak came to an end on March 19, 1989.

success in the Road Runner. Petty's average finish when racing the Plymouth was 3.7. He won four more races in the Road Runner, meaning all eight of his victories were in the older and more reliable Plymouth.

When racing in the Dodge, Petty's average finish was 5.45, with his best finishes being second place (three times) and third place (three times). Overall, the two cars did what Petty wanted them to do, which was to lead him to the first Winston Cup championship and back-to-back titles.

The 1973 season saw Petty race full-time in the Dodge. It was the first time Petty didn't race in a Plymouth during a season since his one-year experiment with Ford in 1969. As was the case the previous season, the Dodge didn't perform as well as the Plymouth. Petty recorded only six victories, the fewest number of wins since 1965, when he missed most of the season due to the Chrysler boycott. Of course, one of the reasons for the fewer wins was the lower number of races. Only twenty-eight races were held in 1973, so Petty's winning percentage wasn't far off from his percentage in 1972.

But the difference was enough to keep Petty from winning a third straight title as he came in fifth. However, Petty did win the Daytona 500 that season, giving him a total of four Daytona 500 titles. The race was a duel between Baker and Petty, as was often the case when the two men raced. The difference between winning and possibly losing for Petty was a pit stop he had toward the end of the race.

"Buddy and I raced each other, and he was probably better than I was. We made a pit stop at the last of the race and then he made his pit stop and as he went back out on pit road, I think we went by him. And then he over-revved his engine trying to catch up and [blew] his motor right there with about 10 or 12 laps to go. Basically we beat him in the pits. We made a better final pit stop than he did."[2]

BACK ON TOP

Missing out on the Winston Cup title in 1973 did not sit well with Petty. The six wins were nice, but his inability to rack up a high number of top-five or top-ten finishes hurt his chances of winning the title as the series rewarded consistency as much as it did victories. Petty wanted to make sure he was more consistent in 1974. It was a goal he achieved.

Petty was better in all areas in 1974. He won ten of the circuit's thirty races, an increase of four from the previous season. He also had twenty-two top-five finishes and twenty-three top-ten showings, an increase of seven top-five and six top-ten finishes compared to the previous season. What Petty couldn't do better was improve his showing in the Daytona 500. That is because as the defending champion, all he could do was match his first-place 1973 finish. He did just that. Petty claimed his fifth Daytona 500 title in 1974, thanks to some bad luck for Donnie Allison.

"Donnie Allison and myself wound up probably being the best cars, but I blew a tire coming off the fourth corner. We were pitting in the first pit stall, and we had installed disc brakes on the front of the car—we were the first ones to have that—and we [were] able to stop in the pits. When we got going again, we [were] still in the same lap, but Donnie was long gone. And not too many laps after that, Donnie blew a tire right past pit road, so then he had to limp all the way around with a flat tire and that just left us all by ourselves. In that deal, we [were] unlucky to have trouble, but lucky to overcome it."[3]

When Petty dominated the field in 1967 with his twenty-seven victories, it was a season that many said could never be duplicated. For the most part, it never will since a fewer number of races are run now. Petty won 56 percent of those races and finished in the top ten in 83 percent of them. In 1975, Petty nearly equaled

DID YOU KNOW? **Petty was named the National Motorsport Press Association's Driver of the Year in both 1974 and 1975.**

those amazing numbers. He won thirteen races and had twenty-one top-five finishes and twenty-four top-ten finishes. Those numbers are close to what he did, percentage-wise, in 1967. Petty won 43 percent of his races in 1975 and had a top-ten finish in 80 percent of his races.

About the only thing Petty did not do in 1975 was win the Daytona 500, as he came in seventh. But he won the World 600 for the first time and his thirteen victories set a record for the modern era, a total that has been matched only once, in 1998 by Jeff Gordon. The Winston Cup title capped an unprecedented run. Petty racked up four titles in a five-year span. From 1970 through 1975, Petty won seventy-six races, or 39.5 percent of his career total. By comparison, Petty won a total of 101 races during the entire decade of the 1960s and would add only twenty-three more victories over the next seventeen years.

TRAGEDY AT THE TRACK

During a race in 1975, Petty came in for a pit stop as his overheated wheel bearing was on fire. Brother-in-law and crew member Randy Owens bolted over the wall with a pressurized water tank in an effort to put the blaze out. However, when the valve was opened, Owens was killed when the canister exploded and sent him through the air.

ONE FINAL TITLE

From 1976 through 1978, Petty had to take a back seat to another driver. Cale Yarborough claimed three straight Winston Cup titles. It wasn't as if Petty fell off the face of the earth. "The King" finished second in the points race in both 1976 and 1977, winning three and five races respectively, and was sixth in 1978. Yarborough was just a little better. Petty, however, still had his share of thrilling races.

Perhaps none was more thrilling than the 1976 Daytona 500. As the race unfolded, it came down

to a sprint between Petty and David Pearson, a long-time rival of Petty and winner of Grand National titles in 1966, 1968, and 1969. The pair were neck-and-neck on the last lap when they entered Turn 4. With the finish line coming quickly, Petty tried to move past Pearson coming out of the turn. Before completing the pass, however, Petty's rear bumper clipped Pearson's front bumper, sending both racers spinning out of control and off the wall.

"For a bizarre moment," wrote the *Washington Post*'s Dave Kindred, "it seemed Petty would win his game's biggest prize spinning backward under the checkered flag."[1]

Petty's car finally came to a stop just yards from the finish line. Pearson bounced off the wall and then hit a second car. But unlike Petty, Pearson's engine was still running and he was able to crawl to the finish line, passing a stalled Petty on the infield grass to win the race and leave Petty with a second-place finish.

The 1977 Daytona 500 wasn't nearly as thrilling for Petty. He looked strong during qualifying and he started the race in third. A victory was not in the cards, however. Engine failure sent him to a twenty-sixth place finish.

He would go on to win five races and finish in the top ten twenty-three times out of thirty races.

Petty is all smiles after capturing his fifth Daytona 500 victory on February 18, 1974.

The season left Petty feeling confident he would return to the top in 1978.

Instead of success in 1978, Petty went through his first-ever winless season since joining the NASCAR circuit as a full-time racer in 1960. He entered thirty races that season, and not once did he wind up in the winner's circle. Not only did his win total suffer, he also had only eleven top-five finishes and seventeen top-ten finishes. His sixth-place showing in the Winston Cup standings was his worst since 1961, not counting his boycott-shortened 1965 season. Petty was so discouraged in 1978 with the Dodge Magnum he was driving that he switched to a four-year-old Chevy Monte Carlo after nineteen races. But the move didn't improve anything.

Followers of NASCAR were starting to wonder if they had seen the best of the forty-one-year-old Petty. Was "The King" no longer able to live up to his lofty expectations? Would 1979 see

REVISIONIST HISTORY

If NASCAR used the Chase for the Cup, the current "playoff" used today to determine the champion, back in 1979, the season's thrilling finish wouldn't have been as thrilling. Petty's eleven-point victory over Darrell Waltrip would have instead been a thirty-three point victory over Bobby Allison, with Waltrip finishing fourth.

Petty return to the top or be a continuation of what just happened? Petty could sense that people were questioning him, and that was all the motivation he would need in 1979.

THE KING STILL RULES

The opening of the season did nothing to suggest that change was in the air for Petty Enterprises. Engine problems forced Petty from the season opener and he settled for a thirty-second place finish out of thirty-five cars. But Petty's fortunes changed at the Daytona 500, a race in which he would be involved in another spectacular finish.

Petty and Darrell Waltrip were just hoping to catch A. J. Foyt for third place. As they entered the final lap of the race, Allison and Yarborough were seventeen seconds ahead. Petty was just trying to finish as well as he could, thinking victory was out of the question, knowing that the two could blow their engines and still coast to the finish line ahead of him.

As luck would have it, Allison and Yarborough didn't just blow their engines, the two slammed into each other down the backstretch straightaway. The two drivers and cars bounced off the outside wall and came to a stop on the infield grass. Foyt, who was an Indy-car star who also raced in some NASCAR events, took his foot off the throttle for a split second, and that was all Petty and Waltrip needed to pass Foyt as the yellow caution flag came out. Petty and Waltrip sped to the start-finish line, with Petty crossing first.

It was a race Petty admits involved a lot of luck for him to get the win.

"Now that was really lucky. That was the most unexpected, I'll put it that way," Petty said. "Even with the Donnie deal [in 1974] we [were] still really good, but with the '79 car, we [were] the fourth- or fifth-best car. Donnie and Cale [Yarborough] were just trucking along, and when it came down to the last lap, it was me, Foyt and Darrell Waltrip racing like a son of a gun for third place. We [were] 20 seconds behind, we didn't have a chance.

"We [were] trying to jockey each other and see who was going to finish third, and Foyt came off the second corner and somehow he [saw] the caution and he hesitated and lifted, and me and Darrell were able to get away from him. We just knew we had to get back to the start-finish line, and whoever was first one back was going to be third. And the deal was, as we headed up the backstretch and started in the third corner, to the left, there's the one and two cars down there. Well, we didn't change our strategy. We [were] still trying to run third. Only thing was, we [were] running for first and second. Coming off the fourth corner, I blocked him to keep him from coming down on the inside of me. I [saw my son] Kyle do that the week before to win the ARCA race."[2]

The Daytona 500 would prove to be a glimpse of how the Winston Cup season was going to play out. Petty would have to rely on a miraculous finish to pull out the Winston Cup title, and just as in the Daytona 500, he was going to get it.

Petty ran well throughout the season, entering the final seven races with three victories and sixteen top-five finishes. Waltrip was having an outstanding season himself and held a 187-point lead in the standings as the drivers headed to Dover with seven races left in the season. It appeared Waltrip was headed for the title, but Petty wasn't about to give up, especially after what happened at Dover.

THE GOLDEN AGE

Many NASCAR fans consider the period from 1964–1979 the Golden Age of stock car racing. Not only was Petty at the top of his game, so too were drivers David Pearson and Cale Yarborough, who each won three Winston Cup titles. Ned Jarrett, Bobby Isaac, and Benny Parsons each won one title apiece.

Darrell Waltrip was one of Petty's main rivals.

FIGHT TO THE FINISH

Petty turned a strong qualifying run into a fourth-place start. Soon, Petty was in the lead and he cruised to the victory, leading for 110 laps on the day. Waltrip, meanwhile, had a horrible day at Dover, finishing in twenty-ninth place. The result allowed Petty to shave

104 points off Waltrip's lead, narrowing the margin to 83 points.

"We were floating along, running decent all year long," Petty said. "About eight or nine races to go [actually seven], we went to Dover. We wound up winning the race, and he fell out. We caught up about half the points."[3]

Just like that, the race for the Winston Cup title was on. The following race took the drivers to Martinsville. Once again, Petty was at the top of his game, as he finished second. Waltrip didn't have the disastrous finish he did at Dover, but he still struggled and came in eleventh. Waltrip's lead over Petty was now down to only forty-eight points. At Charlotte, Waltrip was able to turn his fortunes around, as he came in third. But he didn't gain much on Petty, who placed fourth, allowing Waltrip to gain only five points in the standings.

Waltrip and Petty headed to North Wilkesboro. Everyone was anticipating the event as the two veteran drivers were locked in a head-to-head duel for the title. Petty didn't have a great qualifying session, leaving him in the eleventh position at the start of the race. But "The King" was able to adjust and weave his way through the field for a third-place finish, his fourth straight top-five showing. Waltrip had problems once again and had to settle for an eleventh-place showing.

The lead was now down to seventeen points, and Petty firmly believed the pressure was clearly on Waltrip at that point.

"I remember my favorite racing line of all time," said Chip Williams, a longtime public relations person. "It's getting worse and worse [for Waltrip]. Darrell's leading, but he's falling apart. With about three races left, [the media] asked Richard, 'How much pressure is on you to win the championship?' He said, 'It's kind of like a hound dog chasing a rabbit. The rabbit might be in front, but all the pressure is still on the rabbit.'"[4]

Rockingham was the site of the twenty-ninth race of the year, and there was a feeling of electricity in the air. A good showing from Petty and a poor finish by Waltrip could mean a change in the standings. With his legion of fans cheering him on, Petty claimed the win, leading for 139 of the race's laps. Waltrip, however, raced well and came in sixth. But that was not good enough to hold off Petty in the standings. After a long chase, the hound

ONE TOUGH COMPETITOR

During his career, Petty competed against hundreds of drivers. But Petty said David Pearson was probably the toughest driver to race against, saying Pearson was a better pure driver and was a smart driver on the track.

dog caught the rabbit as Petty claimed the lead by eight points.

The next week in Atlanta, Waltrip would reclaim the lead by finishing fifth, one spot ahead of Petty. But the lead was as close as it could get, as Waltrip carried a two-point advantage heading into the season finale in Ontario, California.

The title came down to one race, and the drivers did whatever they could do to gain a needed point or two during the race.

"We start off and run the race, and we had qualified pretty well," said Petty, who qualified in fifth. "I told [teammate] Buddy [Baker] when we started this race, 'How about letting me lead a lap? That's five points, right?' It worked out."[5]

Waltrip, however, was thinking about trying to gain extra points as well. Unfortunately, one of his strategic moves backfired on him.

"We came in, and Darrell stayed out, to get points," Petty said. "Then they had a caution. They tried to outthink us. D. W. did something he didn't want to do."[6]

Petty captured his seventh NASCAR points title in 1979. It is a record that still stands today.

That move proved costly to Waltrip. It left him one lap off the lead pace and he eventually had to settle for an eighth-place finish. Petty finished the race in fifth place, and after the math was figured out, he claimed the Winston Cup title by eleven points, the closest finish in NASCAR history at the time.

"We weren't doing anything special," Petty said about his mad dash to the title at the end of the year. "If you win the race, you get more points. . . . We didn't have any strategy. It just worked out."[7]

Waltrip admits losing the title down the stretch that season was tough on him.

"The hole got deeper and deeper," Waltrip writes in his autobiography, *DW: A Lifetime Going Around in Circles*. "Ultimately, we blew apart. The failure to win the championship was a crushing blow to me and the team. Losing the title was a terrible thing, but it was a lesson that would help me in the future. We beat ourselves. There is no question in my mind: Petty didn't win it—I lost that championship."[8]

The title was the seventh in Petty's amazing career. It would also be the last time he would be crowned champion.

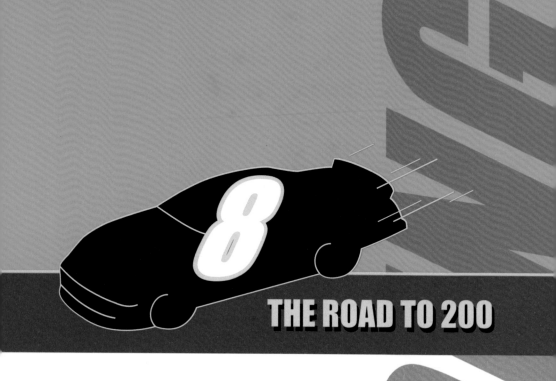

THE ROAD TO 200

With seven championships and six Daytona 500 victories under his belt, there weren't too many things Petty had not accomplished as the 1980s started. Perhaps all that was left to attain was at least one victory in every decade, another Daytona 500 victory, another Winston Cup title, and 200 career victories. Petty didn't earn an eighth championship, but he did accomplish the other three goals on the list.

Petty did not need much time to earn his first win of the decade. He came close at both Riverside and

Richmond as he finished third in those races, and he just missed a victory at Rockingham when he placed second. Those finishes surrounded a twenty-fifth place finish at the Daytona 500, where Petty was knocked out of the race due to clutch problems. In the season's eighth race at North Wilkesboro, Petty finally broke through when he claimed the checkered flag, leading the race for 327 of the 400 laps.

Petty would go on to win just one more race in 1980, but he was competitive throughout the year. He notched fifteen top-five finishes and nineteen top-ten finishes. The consistency he showed on the track allowed him to finish fourth in the Winston Cup standings as Dale Earnhardt claimed his first title.

As the calendar turned over to 1981, NASCAR dictated that the cars had to have a wheel base of 110 inches, a size that car manufacturers had been building since 1979. Petty had experienced success with his Chevrolets and Oldsmobiles, and finished fifth driving a Chevy at the season opener in Riverside. But he decided to go back to Dodge and showed up

DID YOU KNOW?

In December of 1978, Petty underwent surgery in which 40 percent of his stomach was removed due to ulcers. Just two months later, he was back on the track and won his sixth Daytona 500. He won his final Winston Cup title that season.

at Daytona for January testing in a Mirada. While the car looked great, it didn't go fast enough. It was about eight miles per hour (12.9 kph) slower than the cars built by General Motors.

Knowing he would be at a disadvantage on superspeedway such as Daytona, Petty bought a Buick Regal and got it ready for the Daytona 500. It turned out to be a good decision. Petty didn't have the speed some of the other drivers had that day, so he knew he was going to have to win using a better strategy.

"That day, we were probably the fourth- or fifth-quickest car. There was about four or five of us running together, and Bobby Allison had the LeMans and over a period of time, he could get away from the pack," Petty said. "And then in the latter part of the race, everybody had to make one more pit stop. When Bobby came in, everybody else came in, and they put gas in and he took two tires. But Dale Inman said, 'Stay out! Stay out!' So when everybody had made their pit stops, Dale said, 'Come in next lap.'

"I figured we'd get tires and gas, but when we started down pit road, Dale said, 'Gas only!' And I was like, 'We just won the race.' When we went back out, we [were] still leading. Bobby was a lot quicker, but he didn't have near enough time to catch up. So that was just strictly a good call from Dale to win that one."[1]

It would mark the last time Petty would win the event, and it marked the end of an era as Inman, Petty's longtime crew chief, left the team after the victory. The loss of Inman was hard for Petty Enterprises to overcome. Petty did win two more races, one more than he did in 1980, but he had three fewer top-five finishes and three fewer top-ten finishes. The result was an eighth-place finish in the Winston Cup standings.

The 1982 season would be a long one for Petty. He failed to win a race and placed fifth overall in the standings. What hurt Petty throughout the season were poor qualifying runs and a car that wasn't always reliable. Petty's average start in races was thirteenth, a far cry from the days of consistently starting in the top five. For the season, Petty finished only seventeen of the thirty races, and he finished in the top ten in sixteen of those races.

In 1983, Petty's car ran nearly perfectly for him, and he failed to finish only five of the thirty races. Four of those DNFs were due to crashes. He only experienced engine problems one time— at the Daytona 500, of all places. Petty had a great

UNREACHABLE
Just how significant are Petty's 200 career wins? The next closest driver on the career-win list is David Pearson, who won 105 races during his career.

qualifying run and started the race sixth. He held the lead for twenty-nine laps, and it appeared he was going to challenge for his eighth Daytona 500 victory. But his engine blew, forcing Petty from the race and leading to a thirty-eighth place finish.

Two weeks later, Petty won the first of three races that season, taking the flag at Rockingham. He also won at Talladega and Charlotte. For the year, he had nine top-five finishes and placed in the top ten twenty-one times, or in 70 percent of the races. However, Petty's win at Charlotte, the 198th of his career, didn't come without consequences.

After the race that October day, NASCAR officials discovered that Petty had used four left-side tires, an old trick that allowed cars to go a little faster. But it was also against the rules. The postrace inspection also discovered that the engine was twenty cubic inches bigger than allowed.

Petty's brother and crew chief, Maurice, was quick to say he was responsible for the irregularities and that Richard knew nothing of them. But the damage was done. While the win stood, Petty Enterprises was fined a then-record $35,000 and stripped of 104 points. Even worse, Petty left the team his family founded at the end of the season.

Petty was still sponsored by STP in 1984, but he now raced for Mike Curb. There was a noticeable difference in Petty's ability to finish in the top ten. He finished tenth in the overall Winston Cup standings, the first time he wasn't eighth or better in eighteen years. However, the 1984 season is still one to remember for Petty. On July 4, and with President Ronald Reagan in attendance, Petty won his 200th career race in the Firecracker 400. He did it on the track he loved, the Daytona International Speedway.

The win was a thrilling one for the fans to watch as well. With two laps remaining, Doug Heverson crashed to bring out the yellow caution flag. Knowing the race would probably end under the yellow flag, Petty and Yarborough threw caution to the wind and raced to the start-finish line. Yarborough edged ahead of Petty early on the lap, but Petty charged from behind and nipped Yarborough to the line by the length of a fender. The race was Petty's, and afterward, he celebrated in Victory Lane with his family and the president.

No one knew it at the time, but it would be the last victory for Petty as a driver. The following season in 1985, Petty failed to win for the second time in four

A LOT OF RACES

Petty always makes fun of his 200 career wins, saying he lost a lot more races than he won. He is right, of course, as he competed in 1,185 races. For his career, he won only 16.8 percent of the time.

years and had only one top-five finish. It was his worst showing since 1958, when he made his cameo appearance in NASCAR by entering nine races. Petty's fans hoped the good times would return in the 1986, especially when he made amends with Petty Enterprises and returned to the family team he helped make famous. But the return did not lead to any victories. Petty was slightly better in 1987, finishing in the top five nine times and placing eighth in the final standings. But again, there were no victories to celebrate. Petty could still be competitive, but it was clear to many that his days of dominance were gone.

SURVIVING ONCE AGAIN

In his illustrious career, Petty had been involved in numerous crashes. There was the big scare at the beginning of his career, the crash that occurred on the same day as his father's. But many NASCAR fans remember the wreck that occurred in the 1988 Daytona 500, thanks to television coverage of the event. Petty's car tumbled down the track, and many of those watching the trip wondered if he was still alive.

The accident looked much worse than it was. Petty was able to escape with only a sore left ankle, and that injury was due to his car being hit by another car after he came to a stop. But the accident didn't sit well with Petty's wife, Lynda. For the first time in his life, Petty started to think about retiring.

"I was laying there looking at the ceiling and she came in the door. I [saw] she'd been crying but she'd cleaned herself up a little bit," Petty said. "She came in, she looked down, and she said, 'Are we having fun?' Because I'd always told her . . . when I quit having fun driving, then I'm gonna quit."[2]

President Ronald Reagan enjoys a picnic lunch with Richard Petty after Petty won the Firecracker 400 on July 4, 1984.

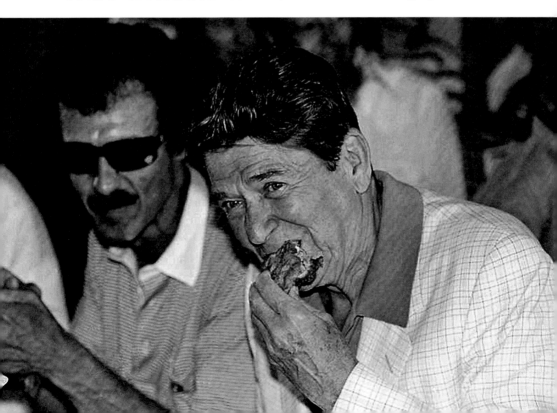

The fun lasted for a few more years, but after experiencing few positive results from 1989 through 1991, in which he had only two top-ten finishes in eighty-three races, Petty announced late in the 1991 season that his 1992 campaign would be the last one in his career. Petty could have taken it easy in 1992, racing in a few select races. That was not his style, however. If he was going to race, he would race a full schedule. But during the entire season, he experienced a year-long Fan Appreciation Tour, which allowed

Petty's car flips down the racetrack after a collision in the Daytona 500 on February 14, 1988.

fans throughout the country to say goodbye to the legendary driver.

A FINAL FAREWELL

The goodbye tour started at Daytona. Petty started the race from the thirty-second position and was able to make a move through the field during the race. But on the ninety-third lap, he was involved in a crash when, trying to avoid the out-of-control mess in front of him, he was hit from behind and sent onto the infield grass. Petty was able to return to the race, but the sixteenth-place finish was not what he had hoped for.

"Yeah, I'm disappointed," he said. "I got stuck in the wrong pack early on, and then I got hit from behind. I didn't see what caused it, but guys get excited and try to drive three abreast."[3]

Petty showed some of the magic that had made him "The King" by qualifying in second for the Pepsi 400 at Daytona. With President George H. W. Bush making a visit on that July 4 day, Petty started strong and led for the first five laps. But he soon dropped out of the lead and on Lap 84, he left the race due to fatigue.

"I'm like a football player who is what you might call over the hill," Petty said. "You've done your thing. I don't know that it's physical as much as mental. All the demands on your time. You're thinking about your fans, about the team, about the sponsor, and you get away from what you do—driving."[4]

The rest of the season progressed slowly, with Petty receiving standing ovations at each track he would visit for the last time. Racing at the age of fifty-five, the season took a mental and physical toll on Petty. But the legend made sure to sign as many autographs as possible and, just as importantly, he qualified for every race.

With the final race of the season—the Hooter's 500 in Atlanta—approaching, Petty was under intense pressure to qualify since he would not get a provisional starting position for the race. As always, Petty rose to the challenge and posted the thirty-ninth fastest time out of the forty-one car field.

The fans packed the grandstands for the race, 160,000 strong. But there would be no miracle ending to Petty's career. No one last hurrah. Instead, Petty was involved in a crash on the ninety-fourth lap, and his

LUCK AND TALENT EQUAL VICTORIES

Petty has always admitted that some of his wins were due to luck just as much as his skill. One example was in the 1981 Daytona 500. Bobby Allison led 117 of the laps and appeared to be in control of the race. But with twenty-seven laps remaining, Allison's car ran out of gas, allowing Petty to go on and win the race.

The final race of Richard Petty's long career featured a crash on November 15, 1992, at Atlanta Motor Speedway.

car caught fire. Climbing out of his car, it appeared his driving career would end right there, with his car smoking due to the flames. But thanks to the work of his crew, Petty's car was repaired enough to allow him to return to the race with two laps remaining. He didn't win the race. In fact, he finished thirty-fifth. But he did finish his career by crossing the finish line with a running car.

"You'd like to go out in a blaze of glory," Petty said. "I just went out in a blaze. Wasn't a whole lot of glory involved."[5]

Petty ended his role as driver in 1992, but he didn't end his involvement with NASCAR. Petty just shifted his competitive nature from driving to being a full-time owner for Petty Enterprises. It was a move that wasn't easy. As a driver, Petty had control over the success of his car as well as the team. But Petty had to get used to seeing his success depend largely on the crews and drivers working for Petty Enterprises.

From 1993 through 1995, Petty Enterprises drivers failed to win a race. In 1993, Rick Wilson recorded only one top-ten finish. Wally Dallenbach, Jr. increased the fortunes of Petty Enterprises in 1994 by recording one top-five finish and three top-ten finishes.

Bobby Hamilton joined the team in 1995 and produced three solid seasons. His first year produced four top-five and ten top-ten finishes to finish four-teenth in the Winston Cup standings. Hamilton then produced the first win for Petty Enterprises since 1983 when he claimed one victory in 1996. He finished ninth in the standings that year. Hamilton would add one more win in 1997 and John Andretti had one victory in 1999. That was the last checkered flag won by a Petty Enterprises driver entering the 2008 season.

The good news for Petty during this drought was the return of Kyle Petty, Richard's son, to Petty Enterprises. A member of the team when he first joined the NASCAR circuit in 1979, Kyle remained with the family operation through the 1984 season before leaving. After more than a decade away, he returned in 1997 and was able to finish fifteenth in the points standings.

In 2000, Adam Petty, the grandson of Richard, appeared in one NASCAR race for Petty Enterprises when he drove the

TOP CIVILIAN
In 1992, Petty received the Medal of Freedom from President George H. W. Bush. It is the highest civilian award in the United States.

No. 45 Sprint car in the DirecTV 500 in Fort Worth, Texas. Adam finished fortieth after being forced from the race on lap 215 due to engine trouble. It would be the last race in which he would appear for his grandfather's team.

PERSONAL SORROW

On May 12, 2000, Adam Petty, who was only nineteen years old, died of head injuries after a crash during a Busch Series practice at the New Hampshire International Speedway. It was a tragedy that shook the entire Petty family. Eventually, Richard Petty was able to come to terms with the death of his grandson.

"When my grandson Adam died, I was more than upset," Petty said. "You say, 'Okay, my father [did] this, I [did] it, Kyle [did] it, and then Adam was doing it and he gets killed.' I set down one night thinking about all this stuff, and I was reading the paper at the same time, and I said, 'You know, part of this is my own fault. If I hadn't encouraged him.' . . . And then I saw two different articles: Fourteen-year-old got killed in a boating accident on a Sunday afternoon, playing around. Another kid, seventeen years old, drowned playing around in the lake. And I said, 'Okay, that's it.' . . . To Adam, it was playing. A nineteen-year-old kid in a race car, having a big time. He died enjoying what he was doing."[1]

Adam Petty (center) celebrates his win in the Easy Care 100 with grandfather Richard (left) and his father Kyle.

Helping the family get through the tough times were all the kind words from fellow drivers. "I think you see very few 19-year-old kids that have touched as many people as what Adam has," Petty said. "The best memory anybody could have is that, hey, he was a pretty good kid."[2]

After talking about it for the first time with the media, Petty said it was time to "move forward," since that is all one can do. "Really, I would just rather everybody forget about it—just have their good memories and then go on down the road," said Petty. "That's what we're trying to do. . . . Right now, we're just re-evaluating everything we had because, as everybody knows, we were putting a lot of future and a lot of things in the basket with Adam to sort of carry the torch for us."[3]

Putting Adam's death out if their minds was not easy, however, because the family was still trying to get over the passing of Richard's father, Lee. The patriarch of the family passed away on April 5 of that year at the age of eighty-six.

"I know everybody has been through this from time to time," Petty said. "As long as everybody stays busy, everybody's doing good. Kyle [Richard's son and Adam's father] has been real, real busy trying to put everything else together."[4]

DID YOU KNOW?

Petty was named the American Auto Racing Writers & Broadcasters Association Man of the Year in 1995 for his contributions on and off the track.

ON WITH THE RACING

The Pettys were able to move on and slowly life started to return to normal. Unfortunately, so did the tough times on the track. Kyle Petty and John Andretti managed to combine for only three top-ten finishes in

2000 and the struggles continued for the next few years. Needing a change in direction, Petty turned to an old and trusted friend in 2004. He brought in Dale Inman, who was Petty's crew chief for 193 of his 200 career wins, to act as an advisor.

"He's got a talent of getting people to work together, all going in the same direction," Petty said. "And everybody here knows what he's done and respects that, so they listen to him. Now, they might not

HE SAID IT

"Oh yeah, we won three or four races here; a couple of the 600s, couple of the 500s. Right now, it's probably arguably the second largest race we have; Daytona's the biggest race, and the way I look at it the [Coca-Cola] 600 is the second, and the 400 at Indy is probably the third as far as prestigious-wise. And it's kind of a big deal, at least it has been since we've been around; we started back in the '60s. It's close to home, and everyone likes to run here, too, cause it's close to home.

"All these trucks out here are probably in a 50-mile radius, so it's everybody's home track; it's one of those kind of deals. It's like coming home; I've never really liked the track that much, probably because we didn't win much here. But, for convenience, it's nice 'cause you got your family, and it's big enough to fit all those people."

— **Richard Petty on racing at Lowe's Motor Speedway in Charlotte, North Carolina** always do what he says, but he has them at least questioning what they're doing."[5]

Inman was retired when he received a call from his cousin. It wasn't long before he decided to offer whatever help he could.

"Richard called and asked if I would come help him out," Inman said. "I wasn't sure what I could do for him, but I told him I would. I've got most of my lifetime invested in Petty Enterprises, so I wanted to help if I could."[6]

Inman brought immediate results to the team. Kyle Petty finished twelfth at a race in Las Vegas, his best showing in one year. Jeff Green ran near the front of the pack for much of the race before being knocked out when he was caught in a crash. Kyle Petty said the Las Vegas race was a boost to the confidence of the team.

DID YOU KNOW?

Petty was inducted into the International Motorsports Hall of Fame in 1997 and in the same year was a charter inductee into the North Carolina Auto Racing Hall of Fame.

"Anybody that struggled as much as we have needs days like Vegas, we need all the good days we can have," he said. "We're not going to get all the way back to the top in a few days or a few races. It'll take some time."[7]

Richard Petty is still involved with Petty Enterprises, but Kyle runs most of the operations. At this stage in his life, Richard Petty is able to spend more time reflecting on all he has done during his career. Despite being retired from racing for many years, he still misses the thrill of competing.

"I miss the driving part, but I hadn't driven since '92. But, I had a decent career and drove probably longer than I should have drove as far as being competitive, but I loved to drive so much," Petty said. "It's kind of like a hunter; just because you didn't kill the bear this time doesn't mean you don't go out next time. A lot of times, the hunt is more enjoyable than the kill. And the racing deal is with me . . . I like to get out there and be competitive. That was my hobby and [I] finally had to give it up. And now, I do everything I used to do except drive. But I miss the driving part, cause that's what I liked to do."[8]

AN INSPIRATION IN HOLLYWOOD

Petty and his famous Plymouth from 1970 served as the inspiration for the character "King" in the Pixar movie *Cars*. In the animated movie, King is a 1970 Plymouth Superbird with the distinctive "Petty Blue" paint job, the famous No. 43, and the crossbar wing on the back.

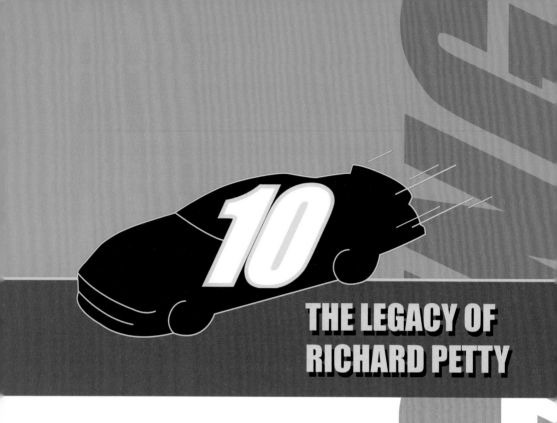

THE LEGACY OF RICHARD PETTY

With his racing career long over and most of the day-to-day operations of Petty Enterprises now run by his son, Kyle, Petty is able to enjoy his life and build upon the legacy he has created. Most of that is done by the numerous goodwill appearances he makes, both for NASCAR and for Petty Enterprises. Petty is also skilled at catering to his loyal fan base.

Earlier this decade, Petty broke out the traditional "Petty Blue" for the No. 43 car John Andretti drove at the time. It was a way to allow the fans to re-member a dominating time of Petty's career.

"The Chex Party Mix No. 43 should bring back a lot of memories for the fans," said Petty. "My Daddy and I started the Petty Blue tradition almost 40 years ago and it will be nice to see a Petty Blue car on the track again at Atlanta."[1]

Petty also has the time to reflect on the changes NASCAR has undergone since his time on the track. Many drivers depend on strategy to win today, perhaps more than on the outright speed of the car alone. The racing fans watch today isn't as "raw" as when Petty dominated the track.

"It's gotten so technical. The cars are so close that you have to depend on gas mileage or you gotta depend on position on the racetrack on a pit stop in order to get yourself in good position," Petty said. "[Back in the good old days] if you had a fast car and you got behind, you just ran hard and you caught up. Racing is where you run up there and beat on some-one, and you get by them and then you go onto the next guy."[2]

CHARITABLE DEEDS

Perhaps what Petty has done best in building his legacy is the charitable causes in which he has been involved. Many are dear to Petty and his family, but one charity means a little more to "The King" than all the others—the Victory Junction Gang Camp.

The camp was started in honor of Adam Petty, Richard's grandson who died in 2000 due to head injuries suffered during a crash at a Busch Series practice. The death was hard on the family, especially since Adam was seen as the heir to the Petty racing throne.

"He was going to be our future," Petty said of his late grandson. "He was the one we were building everything for, the one we were investing in for the long haul. The accident was something our family won't ever fully get over. Adam meant so much to so many people, in and out of racing. You ask why it happened, but never get any answers. That's when you know it's time to pick up and go on. It's hard, and things will never be the same. But you have to pick up and go on. It took the wind out of our sails, but we had to move on."[3]

One way the Petty family moved on was by creating the Victory Junction Gang Camp. The camp, established in October of 2000, is for children with chronic or life-threatening diseases that disqualify them from mainstream camps. Children ages seven to fifteen are offered a one-week stay while their medical and psychological needs are attended to.

"This is something Adam had talked about for almost a year before his accident," Pattie Petty, Kyle's

Kyle Petty holds the trophy aloft to celebrate his first racing victory in 1979 with the Petty family.

wife and the driving force behind the Victory Junction Gang Camp, said. "Kyle and I learned about this type of camp when Bruce Rossmeyer [a philanthropic Daytona Beach businessman] took us to the Boggy Creek Gang Camp near Deland, Florida. That was in 1998, and Adam started talking almost immediately about building a similar camp closer to home for children in Virginia and the Carolinas. People think we founded our camp after his accident. Yes, we started building it after the accident, but we'd started planning it before the accident. Adam was the one who got it started.

We're just carrying on what he would have wanted us to do.

"Of course, things went on hold for all of us after the accident. We'd seen how similar camps had changed people's lives for the better, but we had to wait a while before we really got into this project. . . . We know this is something Adam would have been proud of. For us, it's a labor of love in his memory and honor."[4]

The camp sits on seventy-two acres of land between Randleman and Level Cross in central North

Montgomery Lee Petty leans on her grandfather, Richard Petty, at the announcement of The Victory Junction Gang Camp.

Carolina. Petty and his wife Lynda donated the land, which is close enough to their home that Petty can walk to the camp.

"We looked all over North and South Carolina for enough land that was affordable," he said during the groundbreaking in October 2002. "Finally, Lynda and I decided that what we had right here was exactly what Kyle and Pattie needed. It's our gift to them, our gift to Adam."[5]

The camp is designed to accommodate close to 125 children. Campers and their families are allowed to stay together in cabins and eat at no cost. While the camps are held in the summer, family and sibling retreats and camper reunions are held in the spring, fall, and winter.

"We can do this thing," Petty said at the groundbreaking. "We'll have enough corporate support to open and we'll have plenty of volunteers to keep it going. Obviously, I feel strongly about the thousands of children in Virginia and the Carolinas who will use it. I'm sure Adam is happy with what we've done. It'll be a pretty emotional deal when the first group of kids arrives in June. But it'll be a great deal, too."[6]

More recently, Petty and Kyle did their best to cheer up veterans who are now paralyzed due to injuries suffered in combat. In May 2008, Petty and Kyle visited the McGuire Veterans Affairs Medical Center in Richmond, Virginia. Veterans in wheelchairs showed off their broad smiles as they posed for pictures with "The King" and his son. Just as big were the smiles of the Pettys.

Petty has made several visits to the hospital, and the team announced in November of 2007 that Paralyzed Veterans of America would serve as a primary

THE HAT MAKES A TRIP

Petty is known for wearing his signature cowboy hat. As he often does, Petty takes part in Dodge's satellite conference calls to the men and women of the armed forces who are stationed on the front lines in Iraq. During one conference call, the soldiers commented on Petty's hat. Petty made sure that the soldiers soon received one of his cowboy hats.

"Our soldiers sacrifice so much to allow us to live in a free country," Petty said. "When they asked me to send them one of my Charley One Horse hats I thought that was the least I could do. It meant the world to me that one of my hats could provide them with a little relief from what they deal with on a daily basis."[7]

sponsor for Kyle Petty's No. 45 Dodge for two Sprint Cup races during the 2008 season.

"It makes me feel good that I can generate some happiness for some other people because I'm a pretty happy guy," Richard Petty said. "These are the people that let us go do what we want to do. We can go play, fish, go swimming or run a race car, do our own business on a day-to-day basis and not really worry about the real world that these guys had to go out in. This is our way of saying thank you."[8]

LONG LIVE THE KING

Petty has been able to move on since his retirement and reach out to be

SPEAKING HIS MIND

When asked about Dale Earnhardt, Petty didn't hold back.

"With Earnhardt, he was regular and had a lot of following. Everybody judged everything off of him. He really didn't win that many races. He wasn't that dominant of a driver. He was an exciting driver to watch whether he was running 10th or 13th or leading the race, but he wasn't that dominant when you really get down to it.

"The races he ran against Cale Yarborough or Bobby Allison or Darrell (Waltrip), he was just OK. He was not a standout when you came to that part of it, but he met the criteria the fans wanted in excitement. They could bond to him. That's what carried him."[9]

a positive influence to many people. His charitable work adds to the amazing brilliance he displayed during his racing career. And it is the numbers he put up that will leave a lasting effect on NASCAR. His 200 career wins, his seven points titles, and his seven Daytona 500 victories are the backbone of the Petty legacy.

"When you look at everything he's done, that's the number that kills you," said Kyle Petty. "There's a lot about the history of this sport that you can't compare because the sport's changed so much over the years, OK? But that number—seven wins—stacks up against anything, anytime. That's just staggering."[10]

Petty has not raced since 1992, yet he is still one of the most recognizable faces in NASCAR today. No matter where he goes, people surround him to get his autograph or just talk to him.

And as always, Petty still takes the time to accommodate the fans, something he has done his entire career. He still wears the big belt buckle, the cowboy hat, and the sunglasses. And it always seems he is flash-ing his trademark smile.

"People ask you what your epithet would be," he says. "I say, just to be remembered [is what matters the most]."[11]

Petty won't have to worry about whether or not people will remember him. The King may no longer be racing, but he still rules over NASCAR and leaves behind a legacy that will not soon be forgotten.

CAREER STATISTICS

Year	Rank	Starts	Wins	Poles
1958	37	9	0	0
1959	15	21	0	0
1960	2	40	3	2
1961	8	42	2	2
1962	2	52	8	4
1963	2	54	14	8
1964	1	61	9	8
1965	38	14	4	7
1966	3	39	8	15
1967	1	48	27	18
1968	3	49	16	12
1969	2	50	10	6
1970	4	40	18	9
1971	1	46	21	9
1972	1	31	8	3
1973	5	28	6	3
1974	1	30	10	7
1975	1	30	13	3

Top 5	Top 10	Earnings	Points
0	1	$760	0
6	9	$8,110	4,854
16	30	$41,873	17,068
18	23	$25,239	14,984
32	39	$60,763	28,440
30	39	$55,964	31,170
37	43	$114,771	40,252
10	10	$16,450	5,638
20	22	$94,666	22,952
38	40	$150,196	42,472
31	35	$99,535	2,991
31	38	$129,906	3,813
27	31	$151,124	3,447
38	41	$351,071	4,435
25	28	$339,405	8,701
15	17	$234,389	6,878
22	23	$432,019	5,038
21	24	$481,751	4,783

CAREER STATISTICS

Year	Rank	Starts	Wins	Poles
1976	2	30	3	1
1977	2	30	5	5
1978	6	30	0	0
1979	1	31	5	1
1980	4	31	2	0
1981	8	31	3	0
1982	5	30	0	0
1983	4	30	3	0
1984	10	30	2	0
1985	14	28	0	0
1986	14	29	0	0
1987	8	29	0	0
1988	22	29	0	0
1989	29	29	0	0
1990	26	29	0	0
1991	24	29	0	0
1992	26	29	0	0

Top 5	Top 10	Earnings	Points
19	22	$374,806	4,449
20	23	$406,608	4,614
11	17	$242,273	3,949
23	27	$561,933	4,830
15	19	$397,317	4,567
12	16	$396,072	4,089
9	16	$465,793	4,187
9	21	$508,884	4,450
5	13	$257,932	4,096
1	13	$306,142	3,462
4	11	$280,656	3,765
9	14	$445,227	4,077
1	10	$190,155	2,833
0	0	$133,050	2,432
0	1	$169,465	2,856
0	1	$268,035	3,015
0	0	$348,870	2,971

CAREER ACHIEVEMENTS

- Won a record 200 NASCAR Grand National/Winston Cup races.

- Earned a record seven Grand National/Winston Cup championships (1964, 1966, 1971, 1973, 1974, 1979, 1981) on the NASCAR circuit.

- Won a record seven Daytona 500 races (1964, 1966, 1971, 1973, 1974, 1979, 1981).

- Holds record for most victories in one season—27 in 1967.

- Entered 1,185 NASCAR races.

- Competed in record 513 consecutive NASCAR races (1971–1989).

- Named Winston Cup Rookie of the Year in 1959.

- **Named NASCAR's Driver of the Year in 1971.**

- **Became the first million-dollar winner in 1971.**

- **Named National Motorsports Press Association Driver of the Year in both 1971 and 1975.**

- **Received U.S. Medal of Freedom, the most prestigious civilian honor awarded by the U.S. government, in 1992.**

- **Earned first victory as an owner when Bobby Hamilton won the Dura Lube 500 in 1996.**

- **Inducted into the International Motorsports Hall of Fame (1997).**

CHAPTER NOTES

CHAPTER 1. THE CROWNING OF THE KING

1. "Richard Petty—Joins The NASCAR Circuit," N.D., <http://sports.jrank.org/pages/3722/Petty-Richard-Joins-NASCAR-Circuit.html> (June 1, 2008).

2. Lee Spencer, "Quick Studies," *The Sporting News*, July 19, 2004, <http://findarticles.com/p/articles/mi_m1208/is_/ai_n6142166> (May 29, 2008).

3. Ibid.

4. Ibid.

5. "Richard Petty—1967 season," Auto Editors of Guide, N.D., <http://entertainment.howstuffworks.com/richard-petty.htm> (May 29, 2008).

CHAPTER 2. FOLLOWING HIS FATHER'S FOOTSTEPS

1. Charles P. Pierce, "What I've Learned: Richard Petty," *Esquire.com*, August 1, 2001, <http://www.esquire.com/features/what-ive-learned/ESQ0801-AUG_WIL> (June 1, 2008).

2. Ibid.

3. Ron Frankl, *Richard Petty* (New York: Chelsea House Publishers, 1996), Vol. 1, pp. 21–24.

4. "Richard Petty – 1967 season," Auto Editors of Guide, N.D., <http://entertainment.howstuffworks.com/richard-petty.htm> (May 29, 2008).

5. Frankl, Vol. 1, pp. 21–24.

CHAPTER 3. STARTING A LEGENDARY CAREER

1. "Richard Petty—Joins The NASCAR Circuit," N.D., <http://sports.jrank.org/pages/3722/Petty-Richard-Joins-NASCAR-Circuit.html> (June 1, 2008).

2. Thomas Pope, "Richard Petty: Forever 'The King,'" *The Fayetteville Observer*, February 17, 2008, <http://www.fayobserver.com/article?id=285992> (June 1, 2008).

3. Seth Livingstone, "For The King, Daytona Has Familiar Ring 50 Times Over," *USA Today*, February 14, 2008, <http://www.usatoday.com/sports/motor/nascar/2008-02-14-petty-bonus-cover_N.htm> (June 1, 2008).

4. Ibid.

5. "Richard Petty—Joins The NASCAR Circuit," N.D., <http://sports.jrank.org/pages/3722/Petty-Richard-Joins-NASCAR-Circuit.html> (June 1, 2008).

6. "Racing: Daytona 500 50th Anniversary: Richard Petty," *Daytona Beach News-Journal*, February 14, 2008, <http://www.news-journalonline.com/speed/special/daytona500/richardpetty021408.htm> (May 30, 2008).

7. Livingstone, February 14, 2008.

CHAPTER 4. A QUICK DETOUR

1. Bob Ottum, "Brutes, Brawls and Boosters," *Sports Illustrated*, February 22, 1965, <http://vault.sportsillustrated.cnn.com/vault/article/magazine/MAG1076925/2/index.htm> (June 5, 2008).

2. "Back to the Stocks," *Time Magazine*, February 26, 1965, <http://www.time.com/time/magazine/article/0,9171,833519,00.html?promoid=googlep> (June 6, 2008).

3. Ottum, February 22, 1965.

4. Ibid.

5. Ibid.

6. Ibid.

CHAPTER 5. BACK WHERE HE BELONGS

1. Tom C. Brody, "The Return of The Exile Was Rich and Racy," *Sports Illustrated*, March 7, 1965, <http://vault.sportsillustrated.cnn.com/vault/article/magazine/MAG1078259/index.htm> (June 5, 2008).

2. Ibid.

3. "Racing: Daytona 500 50th Anniversary: Richard Petty," *Daytona Beach News-Journal*, February 14, 2008, <http://www.news-journalonline.com/speed/special/daytona500/richardpetty021408.htm> (May 30, 2008).

4. Ibid.

CHAPTER 6. DOMINATING THE COMPETITION

1. "Racing: Daytona 500 50th Anniversary: Richard Petty," *Daytona Beach News-Journal*, February 14, 2008, <http://www.news-journalonline.com/speed/special/daytona500/richardpetty021408.htm> (May 30, 2008).

2. Ibid.

3. Ibid.

CHAPTER 7. ONE FINAL TITLE

1. "Richard Petty—Joins The NASCAR Circuit," N.D., <http://sports.jrank.org/pages/3722/Petty-Richard-Joins-NASCAR-Circuit.html> (June 1, 2008).

2. "Racing: Daytona 500 50th Anniversary: Richard Petty," *Daytona Beach News-Journal*, February 14, 2008, <http://www.news-journalonline.com/speed/special/daytona500/richardpetty021408.htm> (May 30, 2008).

3. Mark McCarter, "The Final Conquest," *The Sporting News*, April 19, 2004, <http://findarticles.com/p/articles/mi_m1208/is_16_228/ai_n5992810> (May 30, 2008).

4. Ibid.

5. Ibid.

6. Ibid.

7. Ibid.

8. Ibid.

CHAPTER 8. **THE ROAD TO 200**

1. "Racing: Daytona 500 50th Anniversary: Richard Petty," *Daytona Beach News-Journal*, February 14, 2008, <http://www.news-journalonline.com/speed/special/daytona500/richardpetty021408.htm> (May 30, 2008).

2. Thomas Pope, "Richard Petty: Forever 'The King,'" *The Fayetteville Observer*, February 17, 2008, <http://www.fayobserver.com/article?id=285992> (June 1, 2008).

3. George Vecsey, "Auto Racing: Sports of The Times; King Richard Races Last Daytona," *New York Times*, February 17, 1992, <http://query.nytimes.com/gst/fullpage.html?res=9E0CEEDD153CF934A2 5751C0A964958260> (May 29, 2008).

4. Ibid.

5. Mark McCarter, "10 Years After," *The Sporting News*, November 11, 2002, <http://findarticles.com/p/articles/mi_m1208/is_45_226/ai_94334787> (May 27, 2002).

CHAPTER 9. **FULL-TIME OWNER**

1. Charles P. Pierce, "What I've Learned: Richard Petty," *Esquire*, April 1, 2001, <http://www.esquire.com/features/what-ive-learned/ESQ0801-AUG_WIL> (June 4, 2008).

2. Joe Schad, "'The King' Speaks on Losing an Heir," *The Orlando Sentinel*, May 25, 2000, <http://www.accessmylibrary.com/coms2/summary_0286-7266567_ITM> (June 1, 2008).

3. Ibid.

4. Ibid.

5. Keith Parsons, Associated Press, "Inman leads Petty resurgence," *Deseret News* (Salt Lake City), March 14, 2004, <http://findarticles.com/p/articles/mi_qn4188/is_20040314/ai_n11441332> (May 21, 2008).

6. Ibid.

7. Ibid.

8. Steve Chupnick, "Exclusive Interview: Richard Petty Talks NASCAR and Cars," *Movieweb.com*, June 6, 2006, <http://www.movieweb.com/news/87/12887.php> (May 25, 2008).

9. Ibid.

CHAPTER 10. THE LEGACY OF RICHARD PETTY

1. "The Legendary 'Petty Blue' No. 43 Returns to Atlanta Motor Speedway This Weekend," *Business Wire*, November 16, 2001, <http://findarticles.com/p/articles/mi_m0EIN/is_2001_Nov_16/ai_801170 16> (May 27, 2008).

2. Cammy Clark, "Richard Petty Longs for the Good Old Days of Auto Racing," Knight Ridder/Tribune News Service," October 8, 2003, <http://www.accessmylibrary.com/coms2/summary_0286-7552336_ ITM> (May 27, 2008).

3. Al Pearce, "With Class and Style . . . The Pettys Build a Camp for Children with Life-threatening Diseases," *AutoWeek*, December 29, 2003, <http://www.accessmylibrary.com/coms2/summary_0286-19890193_ ITM> (May 27, 2008).

4. Ibid.

5. Ibid.

6. Ibid.

7. "The King's Hat Makes Visit To Iraq," Pettyracing.com, April 15, 2008, <http://www.pettyracing.com/news/article.php?id=227>(May 28,2008).

8. Hank Kurz Jr., "Richard and Kyle Petty cheer up paralyzed vets," USA Today, May 1, 2008, <http://www.usatoday.com/sports/motor/2008-05-01-1659568168_x.htm> (June 3, 2008).

9. David Poole, "Richard Petty just saying what he believes," The Charlotte Observer, June 9, 2001, <http://www.accessmylibrary.com/coms2/summary_0286-8332705_ITM>(May 30, 2008).

10. Thomas Pope, "Richard Petty: Forever 'The King,'" The Fayetteville Observer, February 17, 2008, <http://www.fayobserver.com/article?id=285992> (June 1, 2008).

11. Dustin Long, "The King: He still rules after all these years," The News & Record (Piedmont Triad, N.C.), July 2, 2004, <http://www.accessmylibrary.com/coms2/summary_0286-3766877_ITM>(May 27, 2008).

FOR MORE INFORMATION

WEB LINKS

International Motorsports Hall of Fame:
www.motorsportshalloffame.com

NASCAR Official Web site:
www.nascar.com

Petty Racing:
www.pettyracing.com

FURTHER READING

Blake, Ben, and Dick Conway. *Richard Petty: Images of the King.* St. Paul, Minn.: Motorbooks, 2005.

Bongard, Tim, and Robert Coulter. *Richard Petty: The Cars of the King.* Chicago: Sports Publishing LLC.

Chandler, Charles. *Quoteable Petty: Words of Wisdom, Success, and Courage, By and About Richard Petty, the King of Stock-Car Racing.* Nashville, Tenn.: Towlehouse Publishing, 2002.

Schaefer, A.R. *Richard Petty.* Mankato, Minn.: Edge Books, 2006.

GLOSSARY

caution flag (yellow flag)—Waved when drivers are required to slow down due to an accident or other hazard on the track.

checkered flag—The flag that is waved as the winner of a race crosses the start/finish line.

circuit—An association or league.

crew chief—The manager of a race team who oversees the mechanics of the car and the crew and is responsible for their performance on race day.

draft—The aerodynamic effect that allows two or more cars traveling nose-to-tail to run faster than a single car.

groove—The best route around the racetrack or the most efficient or quickest way around the track for a particular driver.

handling—A race car's performance while racing, qualifying or practicing.

lap—One trip around the track.

manufacturer—A maker of a car or another product.

NASCAR—The National Association for Stock Car Auto Racing, the highest level of stock car racing.

pit crew—The mechanics who work as a team to make adjustments to the car, such as changing tires, during a race.

pit road—The area where pit crews service the cars, usually along the front straightaway.

qualifying—A process in which cars are timed in laps on the track by themselves. The fastest cars get to start in the best positions for a race.

Rookie of the Year—The award given to the best first-year driver on the NASCAR circuit.

short track—A racetrack that is less than one mile long.

sponsor—A business that pays money to a race team, generally in exchange for advertising, such as having its logo painted on the car.

standings—A listing of competitors in the order of their performance.

stock car—A standard type of automobile that is modified for use in racing.

superspeedway—A racetrack that is at least two miles in length.

Victory Lane—The winner's circle where the winning driver parks to celebrate after the race.

Winston Cup—The former name of the championship of NASCAR's highest division.

INDEX